MYTHS AND MYSTERIES SERIES

MYTHS AND MYSTERIES OF NEW JERSEY

True stories
of the unsolved and unexplained

Fran Capo

D1116026

Guilford, Connecticut

To my wonderful boyfriend, Steve—I love you!

To buy books in quantity for corporate use
or incentives, call **(800) 962-0973**
or e-mail **premiums@GlobePequot.com**.

Copyright © 2011 by Morris Book Publishing, LLC

Text design: Elizabeth Kingsbury
Project editor: Gregory Hyman

Map: M. A. Dubé © Morris Book Publishing, LLC

Library of Congress Cataloging-in-Publication Data
Capo, Fran, 1959-
   Myths and mysteries of New Jersey : true stories of the unsolved and unexplained / Fran Capo.
      p. cm.
   Includes bibliographical references and index.
   ISBN 978-0-7627-5993-4
   1. Curiosities and wonders—New Jersey—Anecdotes. 2. Legends—New Jersey. 3. Ghosts—New Jersey—Anecdotes. 4. New Jersey—History—Anecdotes. I. Title.
   F134.6.C375 2011
   001.94—dc22

                                        2010034463

Printed in the United States of America

10 9 8 7 6 5 4 3 2 1

CONTENTS

NEW YORK

Delaware River

Hudson River

Orange
Mountain
▲ ○ CEDAR GROVE
○ WEST ORANGE

NEWARK ○

BASKING RIDGE ○

○ WESTFIELD

MENLO PARK ○

NEW BRUNSWICK ○

Lower
Bay

Delaware River

MONROE TOWNSHIP ○

PENNSYLVANIA

⊕ TRENTON

○ ASBURY PARK

NESCO ○

LEEDS POINT ○

Atlantic

Ocean

DOVER ⊕

Delaware Bay

DELAWARE

| 0 | | 25 | | 50 KILOMETERS |
| 0 | | | 25 | | 50 MILES |

NEW JERSEY

ACKNOWLEDGMENTS

I'm the world's fastest-talking female, so if this were an audiobook, these acknowledgments would go by pretty quickly. But since it isn't, please bear with me. I'll begin with some general acknowledgments, followed by some chapter-by-chapter thanks with a few bonus behind-the-scenes stories mixed in.

First, you wouldn't be reading this if Globe Pequot had not approached me to write this book. This is my fifth book with them . . . so you would be right to assume I love these people! Special thanks go to Meredith Rufino, for working with me so closely, for keeping my voice in the book, and for letting me slide on getting that picture of the New Jersey Devil hitchhiking on the Jersey Freeway with his thumb out and skirt hiked up. Also to the very talented Greg Hyman, my project editor, who was on top of the manuscript to make sure every detail clicked.

Next up, the two most important people in my life: my son, Spencer, who is supportive of everything I do and gives me the best hugs in the world, and my boyfriend, Steve, who even though he is a man and needs to be number one, always gives me my space to write (and have crazy adventures) no matter how long it takes. (He even brags about my adventures later.)

A very special thanks to my dear friend Dale Kilian, whose help was immeasurable in helping me with online and field research, photos, and flips. He accompanied me on treks in all kinds of weather, including a blizzard on the way to the Blue Hole. I also appreciate greatly your encouraging texts as I was on deadline playing beat the clock. You're the best!

I'd like to thank my television co-host, Donna Drake of *Live it Up!,* for offering to help me with research and for introducing me to her friend, Anthony Bruno, photographer. Even though I did not have to take you guys up on your offer, I appreciate it greatly.

I also owe thanks to my friend Lynn Prowse, a virtual assistant, who also offered to help me do research. She's a great gal whom I do teleseminars with and met while I was in Australia.

Thanks go out to my friend Nancy Lombardo for promoting the heck out of all my books on her TV and radio show, *Comedy Concepts,* and to my longtime, honorable friends Ted Isaacson (a proud marine) and Vivian Maltese for having the whole autographed Fran Capo book collection in their libraries. Special thanks to personal business coach Travis Greenlee, who is brainstorming with me to devise even more ways to market this book.

I would like to thank all my Facebook friends who were cheering me on saying "You can do it!" as the stroke of twelve came on deadline day.

And where would I be without my cast of usual characters: Janette Barber, Saranne Rothberg, Ellen Easton, and John

Basedow for always being supportive; also my friends Ruth Borkowski, Patti Roiz, Mike Weinstein, Martha Orellena, Laz Stathes, Dave Farrow, Raquel Benitez and Carmen Llanos from Comet Entertainment, George Bettinger, John Carpenter, Lucy White, Alberto Battaglia, Luis Diaz, Donna McKenna, Roger Paul, Susan Lahoot, Rita Somma, the Capo clan, Dr. Grillo, Dr. Scaperotti and Toni, Aunt Helen, and of course, Mother Mary who helps from above.

Now on to some chapter-specific thanks.

For chapter one, "A Devil of a Son," I want to thank Jan Turner for doing the sketch of the New Jersey Devil when she saw I couldn't get him to pose in person. For "The Friendliest Haunted Castle in New Jersey," my good friend Steven Feldstein invited me into his home, which happens to be his famous private castle, and allowed me write about it, take pictures, and experience the friendly ghosts.

For the Hall-Mills murder chapter, a very special thank you to prosecutor Wayne J. Forrest, Sergeant David Takleszyn, and Michael Wilder of the Evidence Unit of the Somerset County Prosecutors Office for being so gracious to let me see the actual evidence from the Hall-Mills murder case (and, no, I did not touch anything!). They spent over an hour showing me the victims' clothes, diary inserts, fingerprints, etc., and even did a video with me that will be appearing on my YouTube channel, FranCapo1H. It's fascinating . . . look for it. Thanks again, guys. You were awesome!

For the chapter on good ol' Thomas Edison, thanks to my wonderful boyfriend Steve for trekking out there with me to take the photos and do the research and for actually enjoying the trip.

The chapter on the infamous Blue Hole was a doozie! We started out on what we thought was going to be a great day, and it turned into a blinding snowstorm. But did Dale and I turn back? Nooooo! We were determined to get photos and measurements. Luckily for us we were not the only nuts out there that day. As we were trying to find the hidden road in the Pine Barrens, we ran into two local guys, Billy and Dave Arnold. They were nice enough to have us follow their pickup truck to the "real" Blue Hole, not the blue swimming hole commonly mistaken for the real thing. Once they got us to the path, we met what I call the Blue Hole Five, dedicated adventurers like us who were searching for the Devil's Bathtub in the snow as well: Chris Blance, Paul Jordan, Ian Mathisen, Zack Opperman, and Tyler Daniels. Those guys helped us take measurements and carry equipment the half-mile trek on foot, to and from the Blue Hole. But did we stop there? No! Dale and I went back again to take pictures two months later when the weather wasn't so frigid. This time while at the hole we ran into three guys: Chris Berenato (who wants to break a world record), Jerry Melora, and Guy Bucci, who drove Dale and me back to our car from the hole. They have become Facebook and Twitter fans and have promised to help promote this book to all of their friends. (I'm counting on you guys!)

For the chapters on the insane asylum and the Essex County housewives, I want to thank reference librarian Shawn Dempsey and Sharon from the Historical Society of New Jersey for clearing up some questions I had on the facilities.

Researching the Gully Road chapter was a fantastic adventure. On one of the coldest days of the year, I convinced my son, Spencer; his friend Noelia Migueles Abraira; and Dale to join me. Our goal was simply to take some pictures of the haunted road, then head out and hit some other photo ops in Jersey. We found the renamed Gully Road easily enough. We even talked to some local guys, Mario Bermudez and Edwin Medina, who gave us really cool first-person stories of ghost sightings.

After the interviews, since we were near the cemetery, we decided to look for the witch Mill DeGrow's tombstone. We figured, how hard could it be? Four hours later we were still searching. Our hands were frozen. At one point, just to get help in this deserted graveyard, we rang this huge rope bell (the kind like in *The Hunchback of Notre Dame*). We were hoping to find a groundskeeper or someone who had a map or knowledge of the place to help us. No one came. In the process of searching for the tombstone we all got separated. So now not only do we have to find the tombstone, we have to find each other. That took another half hour. Then Spencer lost his cell phone in the graveyard.

We decided to go across the street to try to elicit some help from the City of Newark Police Department. If you walk into a police station and explain you are a writer looking for ghosts and a witch's grave, you will raise some eyebrows.

The officers had not known the history of Gully Street, but history-loving Sergeant Carmine Buonsanto was kind enough to drive us into the cemetery to try to locate the tomb and the missing cellphone. Unfortunately it was to no avail.

A few nights later, Spencer went back, this time with two other friends, Michael Martin and Noelia Silva (yes, he actually knows two Noelias). They searched for five hours. When they got to the oldest part of the graveyard, they started to feel they were being watched. They heard strange whistles, their flashlights started to flicker, and their walkie-talkies would turn on and off by themselves. They decided to take pictures and that's when they spotted the ghostly orbs. In each photo the orbs appeared in different places. As they were leaving the cemetery without the cellphone, Spencer got a strong urge to look in this one spot. There in a spot he had looked several times before, laying on top of a tombstone, was his phone. Creepy? Yes. Now go read the chapter.

For the "Robin Hood of the Pine Barrens" chapter, thanks to my friend Lisa Wernick for research assistance. Thanks also to Bob and Theresa Reilly, who led Dale and me to the Mullica Township police station, where Officer Anthony Trivelli pointed us to the right place.

We owe thanks to the wonderful owner of the house on Pleasant Mills Road, Dorothy Brown-Baldwin. She had no problem with letting me take photographs of the place and also let me do a great flip interview that will be on my YouTube channel.

For the *Morro Castle* chapter, thanks to fellow journalist Don Stine, who was gracious enough to allow me to pick his brain and supplied me with photos. Also thanks to the Asbury Park Historical Society, and Michael Alderson of www.wardline .com; even though I did not use Mr. Alderson's photo, he gave me permission to do so.

Finally, I'd like to thank you, the reader. It's your enthusiasm and quest for information that keeps me writing and employed. If you like the book, please spread the word far and wide to everyone—heck, set up a vending stand. Take out an ad . . . tell your friends, family, Facebook buddies, the FedEx guy . . . just let them know it's out here. I'd truly appreciate it and so would my publisher.

Okay, that's it. Start reading the book!

CHAPTER 1

A Devil of a Son

One dark stormy night in 1735, on a lonely stretch of road called Scotts Landing in Leeds Point, Atlantic County, deep in the Pinelands in South Jersey, an event occurred that would forever haunt and terrorize the people of New Jersey.

Jane Leeds was struggling to bring a child into the world. Her husband, Daniel, was an oysterman who worked the inlets and marshlands of Leeds Point to try to make a meager living. With twelve children already crammed into their small home, Mother Leeds felt she was cursed with this thirteenth child.

As the birth was getting nearer, a midwife and several of the elderly neighborhood women were called in to assist. They all appeared nervous as they waited by the flickering glow of the candle for the child to be born. Maybe it was the thunderstorm outside with lightning ripping through the sky and crashes of thunder sounding like bombs that was making them nervous. Or maybe it was the fact that Mother Leeds was said to have been a witch who had a liaison with the devil himself. But whatever it was, there was an eerie tension in the air.

As Mother Leeds tossed and turned in agony, as many a mother has in childbirth wishing for the child to be born, she yelled, "I don't want any more children. I wish this child be born a devil!" The women looked at each other as chills went through their spines.

Within minutes after that mother's cry, a healthy baby boy was born. Everyone sighed in relief. The women wrapped the baby in a homemade blanket and mother and child smiled at each other.

Then suddenly the baby began to change. The baby's face started to melt like hot molten wax and become distorted. A bone-cracking sound was heard as the once adorable face grew into a horse's snout. Then the body began to stretch and from the shoulders bat's wings sprouted. The body grew longer and longer and stretched into the shape of a humped serpent. Razor-sharp claws sprouted from the hands, horse's hooves sprouted from the feet, and finally a long heavy forked tail completed this demon child.

Everyone watched in horror and disbelief. Then the thing let out its first blood-curdling piercing cry as smoke flared from its nostrils, and it raised its head toward the ceiling. With the birth cry sounded, it turned its head and its red eyes and glared wickedly at the women. They knew they were in trouble. In an instant it was whipping its tail around the room beating the women without mercy. Finally, it turned on its mother, cursing her for cursing him. Satisfied with the bloody damage it had caused, it let out one last cry and flew up the chimney, into the night, and thus began its reign of terror in the neighborhood. And so the demon legend was born.

This is the most widely accepted version of the New Jersey Devil tale, the most famous of New Jersey legends. Since an official proclamation by the legislature in 1939, New Jersey has been the only state to have an official demon.

Since Mother Leeds wasn't taking notes at the time of this child's birth, there is no official record of what actually happened on that fateful night in 1735. Some accounts say that the demon

The Jersey Devil is said to have a horse's snout, batlike wings, razor-sharp claws on its hands, hooves on its feet, a heavy forked tail, and a humped, serpentlike body.

ILLUSTRATION COURTESY OF JAN TURNER

child made its first meal out of two of its brothers and sisters; other accounts say it was really just a deformed child that was shunned and locked in an attic, and then rumors spread. Still others say Leeds had a fight with a local priest who cursed the child. The descendants of the Leeds family will tell you that the Jersey Devil was conceived by the Shrouds family of Leeds Point, the owners of the actual house in which the baby was born. The Shroudses insist the Leeds did the deed. Like Rosemary's baby, this is one son that no mother wants to own up to.

Whatever its birthright, tales of the creature spread panic throughout the Pine Barrens, so much so that it was alleged that the creature was exorcised from the area in 1740. Apparently exorcisms have a statute of limitations, since this one was only good for a hundred years of banishment. Sightings of the creature returned on cue in 1840 and spread as far as New York and Philadelphia.

But the true Devil's lair is in the Pinelands. That's where the sightings began, by people in the area known as the Pineys, who refer to the creature as the Leeds Devil. They held and still hold a solid belief in the demon's existence and a deep-rooted fear. Their beliefs have been reinforced by the many locals who claim to have encountered the Devil.

There were several thousand reported sightings between 1840 and 1999. The New Jersey Devil seems to have a special hatred of animals, for he has been blamed for killing cattle and dragging them away, spooking horses, mutilating German shepherds, and slaughtering chickens. Many skeptics pass these stories off as alcohol-aided fantasy and say a sandhill crane is to blame, but if so it would have to be one particularly evil crane.

Notables throughout the years have also sworn they have seen, or had bouts with, a hellish-looking creature, even in broad daylight. One such notable was Joseph Bonaparte, Napoleon's brother, and the former king of Spain (who hid out in New Jersey for a while). Joseph was said to have spotted the beast while hunting on his estate near Bordentown in the early 1800s. Another respected eyewitness in the 1800s was naval hero Commodore Stephen Decatur, who went to Hanover Iron Works to make sure that the cannonballs being made were the right size and shape for the attacks against the Barbary pirates. While he was lining up a shot on the firing range to test the equipment, in full view and in broad daylight, he saw the Devil flying across the target area. With a steady cool shot, Decatur blasted a hole through the demon. But like any fiery devil does, it simply ignored the wound and went on its demonic way. Those who knew Decatur said he was a respected military man, and if he was lying, that it was the only lie he ever told.

But the most fascinating incident involving the Jersey Devil occurred during January 1909, when thousands of residents from thirty different towns around the Delaware Valley area claimed to have seen the evil fiend.

It started on the morning of January 17 when a Mr. E. W. Minster, the postmaster of Bristol, Pennsylvania, awoke at 2:00

a.m. He looked out his window and saw a creature with a ram's head, long thin wings, and stubby legs. It emitted a cry that "was a combination of a squawk and a whistle . . . beginning very high and piercing and ending low and hoarse," as the *Daily Republican* of Bucks County reported.

The next day a policeman in Burlington sighted what he called a "jabberwock" with no teeth, and eyes like blazing coals, and "other terrifying attributes." Newspapers all around the country began reporting the sightings. Mass hysteria followed.

Strange hoof prints were found on roofs and in backyards. Some claimed to have been chased by the Devil up trees. Others saw the bloody face of the creature up close and personal. In one case a dog in Camden was attacked and the owner reported fending off the beast with a broom. Hunters organized dog posses to try to track down the Devil, but the dogs were too scared to follow in the tracks.

Reports came pouring into the police stations. Schools closed, and people locked themselves in their houses. The papers were dubbing it "the most notorious visitation ever" of the Jersey Devil. An entire fire department was called in on one occasion to shoot a powerful stream of water at a strange creature perched on a roof in West Collingswood. The beast swooped down and the fire crew ran for cover. Many articles were printed in the now defunct *Philadelphia Record* chronicling the Devil's exploits.

By January 22, 1909, mills had closed down in Hainesport and Gloucester County. The demon started making visits to eastern Pennsylvania, and the Philadelphia Zoo offered a $10,000 reward for the creature's capture. Norman Jeffries, a publicity hound and theatrical booking agent, and his friend Jacob Hope, seized this opportunity. According to the *New York Times*, Jeffries "purchased a kangaroo from a traveling circus . . . and painted weird symbols on the animal's head, chest and back and then announced to the world that he had captured the Jersey Devil after a terrific fight in the woods." For added effect, they glued claws and wings to it and claimed it was actually an Australian vampire.

People believed the beast had been captured. But, after a few months, the sightings started again. This time they ended when police found a stuffed bear paw attached to a stick and a sign that read, THE JERSEY DEVIL IS A HOAX. Since 1951, neither the police nor the press has responded to reports of Jersey Devil sightings.

Though the Jersey Devil has been reported slain many times, like Elvis he keeps reappearing. There is even a Web site (http://njdevilhunters.com/sightings.html) with dramatic readings and firsthand video accounts of encounters.

One group, appropriately called "The New Jersey Devil Hunters," has taken on the crusade to prove the legend is true. This group is comprised of several devoted individuals in their twenties, with diversified skills from expert tracking to extensive knowledge of the Devil's antics. Although they have never met the Devil face to face, they feel they have artifacts and strange footprints that prove the demon exists.

The Jersey Devil has been immortalized in lore, feared by generations of adults and children, has had a professional hockey team named after him, and been put on the silver screen in a film called *The 13th Child: Legend of the Jersey Devil.*

While the foundation of the Shrouds house where the Devil and the legend were born can still be found two hundred yards off Scotts Landing Road, skeptics scoff at the tale. But no one has ever proven the New Jersey Devil *doesn't* exist.

CHAPTER 2

The Friendliest Haunted Castle in New Jersey

By the age of thirty, Steven Feldstein was a self-made millionaire. One fateful day he stumbled across a house listing for a stone relic in the *New York Times*. That same day, he received divorce papers. With one chapter closing on his life, he was ready to embark on another one.

Against the advice of his attorney, this self-proclaimed ghost skeptic felt compelled to become the proud owner of Phareloch Castle, a haunted castle located on Shadowbrook Lane in Basking Ridge, New Jersey.

Set on 161 acres of wooded land on the side of Watchung Mountain, the castle itself is at the end of a long, winding, one-lane dirt road in Basking Ridge, in the northeast section of Bernards Township. The recorded history of the town goes back to 1717, when King James III decided to give one of his agents, John Harrison, the equivalent of $50 to purchase the Bernards Township area from the head honcho of the Lenni Lenape Indians, Chief Nowenok. The first settlers to flock into town were

English and Scottish Presbyterians who were escaping religious persecution.

The castle was originally built and designed in 1920 by William Beatty II and his brother, Frank Beatty, to be a retreat for artists. William was an architect and wealthy advertising executive and at one time Frank served double duty as both the Bernards Township mayor and postmaster. With the help of an electrical engineer and some farm laborers, they slaved ten long years over building the castle. It was their utopia and they originally named it Utopia Castle, but then changed it to its later name, Phareloch Castle, after a family crest. The castle's name had Norman origins and first appears in the annals of English history in A.D. 1066. The name was a notable one in the Beattys' part of the world (the county of Herfordshire) and was associated with politics and high affairs in both England and Scotland.

The castle was designed to have twenty-nine rooms, including a great hall forty by twenty feet long with twenty-four-foot cathedral ceilings with hand-applied gold leaf. It also had two towers featuring cone-shaped roofs. And of course, what castle would be complete without its share of winding staircases, secret rooms, and passageways? Stained glass windows imported from France adorned the windows, and handmade floor tiles from Finland and Portugal finished off the elegant look. The roof was made of slate that cost $35,000. The total cost of their dream castle was $150,000.

Six months before the castle was finished, William, his wife, Sarah, and their four children happily moved in. But tragically, William died from a strep infection in 1931 before it was completed. He passed away peacefully in the master bedroom, and services were held in one of the towers.

Shortly after his death, his wife started seeing his ghostly form on the balcony and in the ballroom. The groundskeeper even told her that he would often see him lingering on the stairwell. He was obviously not ready to leave his home. Sarah, Beatty's widow, conducted numerous séances in the castle to try to contact her departed loved one and said she communicated with him on occasion.

Sarah stayed on in the castle until the mid 1950s. Eventually, the house became too large for her. She moved to Westfield, New Jersey, before her retirement to Florida. But apparently Bill Beatty stayed behind, guarding his beloved castle.

In 1959 the castle was bought by Joseph Bauernschmidt of Long Island. But he apparently was more interested in owning the land than maintaining the opulent castle. He left the place vacant, and observant vandals took it upon themselves to break one hundred windows, rip out light fixtures, and for good measure, smash the plumbing.

The home, or what was left of it, was sold again, this time to a woman by the name of Kathryn B. Crofts, who decided to leave the castle on eight acres, and set aside 142 acres for other purposes. At one point she converted the large cathedral living room into an antique shop. After a few years, she grew tired of the castle and sold it in 1965 to two builders, Andrew Woehrel and Al Grosh, who bought it as an investment.

In 1970 Woehrel and Grosh decided to lease the castle out as a private school known as Chartwell Manor, or the Woodcastle School for Boys. The school was not a safe haven for the youngsters, however. Students started to report seeing ghostly beings in the hallways. Apparently their claims were dismissed as just the imagination of children. Luckily for them, though, their other claims were not ignored. The headmaster, "Sir" Terrence M. Lynch from Scotland, was taking liberties with the boys. He was later convicted of molesting his students and to this day is serving jail time for that and for molesting three adults. The school was closed one short year later and relocated to a new campus in Mendham, New Jersey.

The castle was seemingly on a run of bad luck and the owners wanted to sell it. In order to unload it quickly, they decided to spruce up the place. One of the owners, Andrew Woehrel, had his son and two friends help him paint the inside of the castle. Feeling that the boys could handle the job, Woehrel left them alone to work. The boys stayed at the castle, painted for a while, and when they got tired, went to sleep in their sleeping bags near the fireplace on the first floor. Apparently they were too close to the fireplace and ashes from the fire jumped onto the sleeping bags, igniting the floor panels. The fire quickly got out of control and destroyed 80 percent of the castle. All that was left were the eighteen-inch stone walls and steel beams; not even a roof remained. The pipes were exposed, and charred remnants were everywhere. Luckily, the boys escaped in time.

With not enough money to hold on to the castle or to repair it, Woehrel and Grosh declared bankruptcy and in 1971 the remains of the once beautiful castle were bought at a sheriff's auction by Donald Burlingame and his wife, Carol, for a mere $43,000.

The Burlingames thought they had obtained a steal on the castle and eagerly started rebuilding it. First, they gutted the entire dwelling by carting out 125 barrels of debris by hand and replaced the roof and walls. They also started the rebuilding of the seven-room servant cottage in the back so they could have a place to live. The number of rooms in the castle was reduced to twenty-one from the original twenty-nine. While some owners might have been mostly interested in the land and would have torn down the castle to build a modern, energy-efficient house, Burlingame was excited to own one of the last standing castles in the county. He seemed to love it just as much as Beatty did.

Burlingame lovingly reconstructed the castle from photographs and tried to restore it to its original grandeur. But as each owner soon found out, a castle is not an easy thing to rebuild or maintain, especially when you're being watched by the original owner. The ghost of "Ole Bill" Beatty decided to make his presence known by closing the windows during rainstorms. Maybe he was making sure his beloved home was being kept dry. But he didn't stop there.

There were mysterious knocks on the front door, and when the Burlingames went to answer, no one was there. Doors would also open and close by themselves. Television sets would change channels themselves, footsteps could be heard coming down the stairs, puffs of smoke rose and disappeared from the floor, organ music could be heard coming from the basement in the middle of the night, pictures would dance on the wall, loaves of bread would fly off the counter, and a pet kitten that was left out at night would be back in his cage with the latch sealed in the morning. Car windows would even go up and down by themselves near the castle.

The ghost was getting bolder. He even appeared to the Burlingames' tenant outside the home dressed in a gray business suit. When the tenant asked the "man," "Can I help you?" Bill faded before his eyes. The tenant screamed as he ran to tell the Burlingames of his encounter. Even the Burlingames' dogs and cats got into the act. They noticed the ghost as well, as they would growl at vacant rocking chairs as if someone were sitting in them.

The Burlingames decided to bring in some psychic investigators to see what was happening. The psychics confirmed the ghostly energy, saying that "he [Bill] probably won't leave here because it's unfinished business for him." At one point in 1974 they were going to do an exorcism but ruled it out, saying the ghost was a friendly one.

Carol said she told the ghost he could stay under one condition—that he never actually appear to her. She said, "If I ever see you, I'll probably end up in a padded cell."

Apparently Bill kept his end of the bargain, and they all lived in harmony together. Carol and Donald didn't mind his presence. While Carol didn't want to see him, the husband said to one reporter that he was actually hoping Bill would make an appearance during one Halloween party they were holding.

The house and its original occupant started getting some notoriety and in 1982, the ABC television show *That's Incredible* did a segment on it, thrusting the ghost into the spotlight. On October 20, 1984, a local New Jersey paper did a story on it as well. It went on to get more press and was featured in numerous newspaper articles with headlines like: GHOSTLY TALES NOT ALL FOLKLORE, CASTLE LOVER LOOKS FORWARD TO "CAMELOT," CENTRAL JERSEY CASTLE HAS THINGS THAT GO BUMP IN THE NIGHT, SOME MEN'S HOMES REALLY ARE CASTLES, and TV PROGRAM SPARKS INTEREST IN LOCAL "HAUNTED CASTLE" FOR SALE.

The Burlingames spent eight years restoring the castle. They stopped work on the project in 1993, sold it for $795,000, and moved to Costa Rica.

Bill the ghost bid goodbye to the Burlingames and once again the castle changed hands. This time, the castle was purchased by the Peacock family. After seven years of living there, they decided to place the ad in the *New York Times*, the ad that the current owner Steven Feldstein saw.

Feldstein loves the castle so much he decided to set up his office by a stone fireplace inside it. He lives in the finished side of the castle. The side that was destroyed by the fire is covered in a blue tarp. That section is still being restored and is the place where curious, personally invited spectators can have their ghostly encounters.

Steven is skeptical by nature and was content to just live in the castle without question. But when his son Brenton told Steven that he saw a strange man in the castle, Feldstein became curious. Then Brenton told his father he had a conversation with the man who identified himself as "Willy," a name Bill Beatty's

PHOTO COURTESY OF D. V. KILIAN

Present-day Phareloch Castle, renowned for being home to over thirty-seven friendly ghosts. A fire in the 1970s destroyed a large portion of it. The current owner, Steven Feldstein, is having it refurbished to bring it back to its original grandeur.

friends and family used to call him. In addition, Steven's then-girlfriend, Susan, an artist, was certain Bill existed and even took some pictures where ghostly orbs appeared. Steven decided there might be something to their claims, and became determined to get to the bottom of the mystery.

Over the years, Steven welcomed many psychic investigators into his home to see if they could help him become a believer. The NBC show *Unsolved Mysteries* even came in to check it out. Both the psychics hired by the show and independent psychics brought a wide array of ghostbuster tools and picked up some thirty-seven positive energies, making it the most friendly haunted house in all of New Jersey. Hey, why not? There are plenty of rooms in the place!

To remind visitors that the castle is a private home, Mr. Feldstein established a set of guidelines for those invited inside. These guidelines are to protect his ghostly occupants. The rules were laid out as follows: "Please use no spells, incantations, lines of questions that either anger [them] or insist that the ghosts follow you home. They need to remain in the castle." The guidelines continue, ". . . and please, no opening of portals of any kind . . . we don't want the Stay-Puft marshmallow man from *Ghostbusters* showing up. Sensing equipment, like dowsing rods, pendulums, EM field sensory devices, etc., are not only allowed, but also appreciated."

Feldstein invited the South Jersey Ghost Research Team (SJGR) to perform an investigation of the castle with a team of six people on September 26, 2004, from 8:45 p.m. to 11:45 p.m.

During that time they took 715 photos throughout the house. They noticed that the ballroom section seemed to be the center of paranormal activity. As they reported, "Many of the investigators were touched and tapped many times in this area. The scent of alcohol was picked up upon the walkthrough prior to us being told that it used to be a ballroom. The spirit of a soldier was also obtained in the ballroom and appeared to be frightened and lost. The team also obtained some positive photos and an EVP. There were also 2 EMF fluctuations that could not be explained or traced to a natural source."

(Note: An EVP [Electronic Voice Phenomenon] device records audio during ghost hunting investigations. Human vocal cords are capable of making sounds within the 300- to 3,000-Hertz range. Many paranormal researchers attribute recordings outside this spectrum to be spiritual. EMF stands for Electromagnetic Field. An EMF meter reads the fluctuations in electromagnetic fields created by power lines, appliances, etc. Typical readings in a home are from 9.0 to 30.0. Anything that registers in the 2.0 to 7.0 range and cannot be traced to a source is attributed to spirit activity.)

With their sophisticated instruments, the team picked up a tremendous amount of residual energy and photographed a number of orbs.

Despite any ghostly presence detected by the team, Steven was dedicated to living in the castle, and his then-girlfriend, Susan Ridley, liked the spiritual energies, since she felt they were all positive. She said, "Ghosts are just another way of being, and if you show them respect, they will in turn respect you."

To date, Steven has not seen any entities himself. He sums it up by quoting Napoleon: "Glory is fleeting, but obscurity is forever." He allows people in his home because he wants to be a believer in the spiritual realm. He wants people to prove the presence of ghosts, both to themselves and him.

One thing is for sure though. If the ghost of Bill Beatty does reside in the castle, he has certainly had the last laugh: After all, he has lived rent-free for almost a century.

CHAPTER 3

The Minister and the Choir Singer

A t 10:00 a.m. on the sunny Saturday morning of September 16, 1918, an excited young couple, fifteen-year-old Pearl Bahmer and twenty-three-year-old Ray Schneider, decided to go for a little secluded walk and maybe hold hands along the way. Their destination was the abandoned Phillips farm off of De Russey's Lane, which is close to the border of Middlesex and Somerset Counties. What they got instead of a romantic romp was a surprise that wound up shocking the nation.

There, under a crabapple tree, lay two decomposing bodies: one of a man and one of a woman. The couple lay on their backs with their feet facing toward the crabapple tree. The woman was dressed in a blue dress with red polka dots and black stockings. Her head was resting on the man's shoulder; her left hand was resting on his right knee. A brown scarf covered the lower part of her neck, which had been slashed with a knife from ear to ear so deep it was down to her spinal cord. Her head was almost off. Everything was cut but one muscle, the backbone, and a few inches of flesh. She had also been shot three times: in the right temple, under the right eye, and over the right ear. Her tongue had been cut out and her larynx had been removed. One of her arms was bruised and there was a small wound on her upper lip. The man was not as badly treated; he was only shot once over the right ear. His face was covered with a Panama hat, his right arm was under the woman's shoulder, and a small business card, his own, was leaning against his left shoe.

Some torn pieces of paper and handwritten cards were scattered between the bodies. One read, "Oh honey, I am fiery today. Burning, flaming, love." Another sizzled with, "There isn't a man who could make me smile as you did today."

A man's dark leather wallet was lying open near the bodies on the ground. There was no sign of struggle, but the grass near the bodies had been recently trampled on as if someone had placed the bodies there. They had been dead for about thirty-six hours and a .32-caliber bullet lay nearby.

The young couple ran across the field to the home of Edward Steryker. They blurted out the story of their gruesome find and Steryker's niece, Grace Edwards, who overheard the story, called the New Brunswick police at 10:30 that morning. Five minutes later, officers Edward Garrigan and James Curran were on the scene and were questioning Pearl and Ray.

The press got wind of the story and Albert J. Cardinal from the *New Brunswick Daily Home News* joined the officers on the scene. He was given permission to pick up the business card by the dead man's foot. His action tainted the first piece of evidence with his fingerprints. Next on the scene was Lieutenant Dwyer with a local veterinarian, Dr. Leon Loblien. The vet identified the bodies. By then it was becoming a free-for-all. The story spread quickly and more press and curiosity seekers arrived, all of whom contaminated and almost completely destroyed the crime scene evidence, laying the groundwork for this to become one of the most complicated murder cases in New Jersey history.

Forty-five minutes later, after being temporarily sidetracked by wrong directions, Detective George D. Totten from the Somerset County prosecutor's office, along with Sheriff Bogart Conkling, and a county doctor, William Long, arrived.

Now here's where it began to get sticky, as nobody was sure where jurisdiction would lie. Because the corpses were found in Somerset County, the New Brunswick police notified Totten's office, but it seemed apparent that the couple wasn't killed where they were found. Would jurisdiction lie where the bodies were found or where they were killed? This issue would eventually cause a lot of problems with who would hold the evidence as the case unfolded.

The crime scene in Somerset County was now a madhouse and a nightmare for detectives. Hundreds of souvenir hunters, sensing this was going to be a big story, had stripped off the bark of the crabapple tree. The underbrush was trampled down with dozens of pairs of feet, people were raking the leaves looking for the murder weapon, and the calling card that was originally by the man's foot had passed hand to hand, making it difficult to determine whose fingerprints were originally on it. As far as the Phillips farmhouse near the tree, people actually tore pieces of the porch off, one person grabbed a windowpane, and the farmhouse's furnishings were ransacked. There were just too many people for the police to control. As the day continued, it got even more bizarre as those with the entrepreneurial spirit started setting up vending stands and selling hot dogs and popcorn to the curiosity seekers.

Luckily, Detective Totten noticed a two-foot-long iron pipe lying close to the dead couple. He also noted several other telltale signs: the couple's clothes were perfectly arranged, suggesting someone had placed them there; the man's eyeglasses were on and spotted; and the business card that had been passed around contained small specks of something. He jotted it all down and wrapped the evidence in a brown paper bag.

So who exactly were this loving couple? The bodies were identified as forty-one-year-old Reverend Edward W. Hall, a slightly heavy, balding minister of the Episcopal Church of St. John in New Brunswick. He was married to none other than Frances N. Stevens, heiress to $2 million from the Johnson and Johnson family fortune. Frances was seven years older than the minister, and not an attractive woman. She was once described as "dumpy, plain, and severe-looking."

The dead woman next to the minister was thirty-four-year-old Eleanor Mills, a soprano in the church choir. Her husband was Jimmy Mills, a mild-mannered man who was the sexton at St. John's Church and never made more than $38 a week in his life. Eleanor and Jimmy had two children, Charlotte and Danny. As the children got older, Eleanor devoted her time to romance novels and the church, perhaps living out her own romantic fantasy with the reverend. Thus the case of the minister and the choir singer began. Up until the Lindbergh baby case (1932), the Hall-Mills murder case would be known as the crime of the century. It contained all the elements of a good scandalous murder mystery: money, love, lust, betrayal, jealousy, bribery, and passion. The press loved it.

After the bodies were identified, around 2:00 p.m. they were loaded into a hearse by Somerset undertaker Samuel T. Sutphen. As Sutphen and an assistant were moving the minister's body at the morgue, another bullet fell out of the holy man's coat. It was secured as evidence.

Reverend Hall's funeral took place on Monday, September 18, at 11:00 a.m. The service was quick and Bishop Albion Knight of Trenton, New Jersey, read more of a press release than a eulogy: "In view of the unfortunate mystery surrounding his death, we do not hesitate to maintain our confidence in his character, entirely unshaken by the evidence so far revealed by public report." During the actual service, people noted that the reverend's wife did not shed a tear, and from that moment on, the press cast her as the "Iron Widow." Forty-eight hours after his body was found, Reverend Hall was buried in Greenwood Cemetery in Brooklyn, in the lowest drawer of the family vault, under the watchful eye of his dead mother-in-law, Mrs. Stevens.

The next day, September 19, Eleanor Mills was laid to rest. Because of the gruesome cutting of her throat and the shots to her face, it was a closed casket service.

Both Mr. Mills and Mrs. Hall claimed they knew nothing of any affair between the deceased. Both also claimed that they felt their respective spouses had been loyal to them. Eleanor's husband, Jimmy, said he believed that robbers killed them for "his gold watch and money." He said he couldn't conceive that an affair was going on because the minister was "his best friend." But even if Jimmy was as simple-minded as he appeared, it seemed odd that he would not know about the love letters Mrs. Mills kept in plain sight in a crocheted bag behind the living room door. In that bag Mrs. Mills also kept a diary dated from July 31 to August 12 that the reverend sent to her upon her request, detailing his summer vacation with his wife in Islesford, Maine. The diary was written for Mrs. Mills's benefit so she could live vicariously through him. Eleanor had also confided in her sisters that she planned on going to Japan and eloping with the minister at some point. Whether Jimmy Mills ever read the contents of the bag would have to be determined in court. For the moment the investigators knew that Jimmy Mills had kept a sharp shoe-cutter knife left over from his shoemaker days. He could easily have slit his wife's throat with it, but there was no evidence linking him, the object, and the murder together.

But love is blind, or in this case, purposely deceitful. Apparently everyone but the spouses claimed they knew about the affair. Indeed, it had been going on for four years, since late 1918. It seemed to be common knowledge that the two had been meeting every afternoon at the Mills house located at 49 Carman Street, and they had often been seen together around town.

So what exactly transpired on that dreadful night up until the time of their death? No one really knows for sure, but at the time suspicion naturally fell on the jilted spouses, Jimmy Mills and Frances Stevens Hall.

Jimmy Mills told the following version of the events of that fateful week. On Thursday, September 14, two nights before the discovery of the bodies, he left the church and returned to his home. The time was approximately 6:15 p.m. It was a tad later than normal and Eleanor was not happy. She complained, "You're late for your supper." Forty-five minutes after Jimmy got home, Eleanor told her daughter Charlotte that she was going to leave a newspaper clipping on the minister's desk. It was an article Eleanor had torn from the *New York World* newspaper by Dr. Percy Stickney Grant, a well-known liberal Episcopal clergyman who believed in divorce.

At 7:15, Eleanor came home, put on her hat, shawl, and scarf, and was about to head out again, this time with Jimmy's knowledge. Jimmy asked where she was going. She replied,

"Follow me and find out!" But Jimmy claimed that he never did. She told Charlotte that she was going to the candy store to call Reverend Hall, claiming that he called her and she needed to return his call. Since the Mills didn't have a phone this was the routine, with one exception: Eleanor usually called from her neighbor Miss Opie's house, but this time she chose to use a pay phone. Ten minutes after Eleanor left, Charlotte and her brother Danny, who were told to stay home and wait for her return, instead left and went to their aunt's house. This was the last time Jimmy and the kids said they saw her.

That night when Jimmy was reading the newspaper he noticed an article had been clipped out. According to Jimmy's accounting of events, when Mrs. Mills had not returned home by 10:00 p.m. (her usual hour), he went to the church to look for her. He couldn't find her so he came home and went to sleep. He woke up at 2:00 a.m. and went upstairs to the attic bedroom where Eleanor always slept with her daughter and realized she still wasn't home. He went to the church again thinking maybe she had had one of her spells and fainted in the pews. There were no signs of her anywhere. When he awoke at 5:45 a.m. on Friday morning, she still wasn't home. When asked by detectives why he didn't call the police he said, "I didn't bother to file a missing persons report because my wife on occasion would disappear for a day or two, so I wasn't worried."

Jimmy said that he had run into Mrs. Hall when he went to the church at 8:30 that same morning, a story separately confirmed by the recently widowed heiress. They said good morning to each other. Then, reconstructing the conversation from versions told by both Mrs. Hall and Mr. Mills, out of nowhere Mrs. Hall asked Jimmy, "Did you have any sickness in your home last night?" He replied, "No." Mrs. Hall continued, "Mr. Hall did not come home all night." Then Jimmy, who supposedly knew nothing of their affair blurted out, "Do you think that they eloped?" To which, Mrs. Hall, who supposedly knew nothing about the murder or affair replied, "God knows. I think they are dead and can't come home." For two spouses who had no knowledge of an affair, it was a rather interesting exchange.

Jimmy claimed that he and Mrs. Hall ran into each other again later that day, and that Mrs. Hall repeated, "They must be dead or they would have come home."

Being a sexton of the church, Jimmy Mills had full access to all areas. As he continued to work around the church he happened upon the missing page from the newspaper he saw at home. The headline of the article on the minister's desk read: EPISCOPAL MINISTER'S VIEW ON DIVORCE. Jimmy claims he only read the headline.

Jimmy said he found out about his wife's death on Saturday, September 16, when he had an early lunch at the home of one of his sisters-in-law, Augusta Tennyson. A reporter called the Tennyson home and said that an unidentified woman had been found dead with the reverend. Jimmy said right away he assumed it was Eleanor. He was going to head to the crime scene, but wasn't sure if the bodies were on Ryder Lane or De Russey's Lane, and by that time he had already stopped at home and spoken to his daughter, who tearfully told him a positive ID had been made. He then rushed to the Halls' home and was so sick they had to give him some ammonia so he wouldn't faint.

Meanwhile, Mrs. Hall had her own story of her whereabouts on the night of the murder. She said that her husband, the minister, was out on that Thursday evening of September 14, distributing flowers to a local hospital with his niece. Eleanor Mills had called and asked to speak to the minister, and she had told her he was not home yet. According to Mrs. Hall, Mrs. Mills gave her a message for the reverend: "You tell him that there is something about the doctor's bill for my operation that I do not understand."

Mrs. Mills called back later when the minister was home. Mrs. Hall picked up the phone at the same time her maid, Louise Geist, picked up. The maid saw her on the extension and Mrs. Hall put the phone down. Then the maid got Mr. Hall from the upstairs bathroom to answer the phone.

Shortly after, around 7:00 p.m. on September 14 according to Mrs. Hall's version of events, the minister announced that he was going to check on Mrs. Mills's medical bill. (Reverend Hall had promised to give Mrs. Mills $50 to help pay the cost of her recent kidney operation.) Mrs. Hall claimed that when Mr. Hall left, that was the last she ever saw of him.

In the house at the time were two maids (Geist and Barbara Tough), Mrs. Hall, her niece, and her brother Willie Stevens. When the reverend wasn't home by 10:00 p.m., she began to worry. At 2:30 a.m. she got up and saw that her husband still wasn't home, so she went to her brother Willie's bedroom and asked him to walk with her the few blocks to the church on George Street. She thought that maybe Mr. Hall had fallen asleep there. As she and Willie left the house she saw that the garage door was open and noticed both the family cars were still there. When the reverend wasn't found at the church, they decided to walk the few blocks to the Mills house to see if they were there. When they saw all the lights were out, they just went home. That Friday morning at 7:00 a.m., she anonymously called the police to ask if any "casualties" had been reported.

Mrs. Hall confirmed Jimmy's report that the two of them had run into each other at church later that morning. Later that afternoon Mrs. Hall telephoned her sister-in-law and her attorney, Mr. Florence. The attorney came to the Halls' home at 3:30 p.m. and told her to file a proper report with the police.

Mrs. Hall claims to have found out about the murders when a journalist from the *New Brunswick Daily Home News,* Al Cardinal (the one who was first on the scene with the cops), called her home and started asking her questions about the whereabouts of her husband. She claims she got suspicious and sent her cousin, Edwin Carpender, down to the office of the newspaper. It was then he found out that the reverend's body had been found under the tree. As word spread, people came forward to tell their stories to the police to help piece together what might have happened.

Both Jimmy Mills and Frances Hall said they believed the motive was robbery. On September 21, Mrs. Hall released a statement to the press via Miss Sally Peters, her maid of honor. "The widow's opinion was that robbery was the motive of the double slayings. Not only had the rector been wearing his valuable gold watch, but he had also carried about fifty dollars in his wallet with which to pay for Mrs. Mills's operation." This theory was plausible because the police had found neither the money nor the watch on Hall's body.

For the next twelve days officials turned up no leads whatsoever. Although the killer's identity remained a mystery, there were several theories that had already been ruled out: one, that the crime was done by thieves (because if they stole for money the gold hunting watch would have turned up at a pawn shop somewhere); two, that blackmailers were involved (because no one came forth to ask for the Mills fortune); and three, that the Ku Klux Klan was responsible. The Klan was quickly ruled out because the police did not see a KKK insignia anywhere near the crime scene, and because they felt there were enough holes in the families' stories to make them the prime suspects.

After some political maneuvering, the investigators decided to exhume the bodies and perform an autopsy. The autopsy didn't turn up much new information, except that Mrs. Mills's throat had been cut after she was already dead. The examiners also took it upon themselves to open up an abdominal scar and found out she was not pregnant.

As the governor was putting pressure on the police to find the murderers, a break in the case came on Sunday, October 8, 1922. After twelve hours of grueling investigation, the police announced the arrest of Clifford Hayes. Clifford was a close friend of Ray Schneider, the New Brunswick boy who had discovered the bodies. Ray said Clifford and his friend Leon Kaufmann were with him on the night of the murders and that they had followed Pearl and a drunken man into the park. Ray said he was going to beat up the man (not realizing it was Pearl's drunk father). He claimed Hayes pulled out a pistol he had been carrying and said he would take care of it. They lost Pearl and the man when they headed into the park. That was at 11:00 p.m. At that point Kaufmann went home. Ray claimed later he and Hayes went back and saw two people, and then Hayes fired four shots thinking they were Pearl and her dad. Ray said he ran from the scene, and he claimed that Hayes later realized it was the minister and the choirgirl. Based on Schneider's testimony, Clifford Hayes was arrested.

The townspeople were up in arms, and they cornered Middlesex detective and arresting officer Frank F. Kirby at a train station and started throwing rocks at him. Many believed the police had pressured Ray Schneider to make a statement just to resolve the murder case. A few days later, Schneider admitted he had lied and Hayes was released. Ray Schneider was then arrested for perjury and the statutory rape of Pearl Bahmer (a charge Pearl's father brought). In turn, Pearl accused her dad, Nicholas Bahmer, of incest, and he was arrested as well. The case was getting messier by the minute. Eventually Pearl was sent to a home for wayward minors and her alcoholic father was released on bail with the incest charge still pending. Ray Schneider was sentenced to two years in prison for perjury but the rape charges were dropped.

A few days later, four good breaks came in the case. First, on Monday, October 16, two blood-stained handkerchiefs that were found on the farm on the day of the murders were turned over to the New Brunswick police by the Somerset County police. One handkerchief was unmarked and the other had a small "s" in the corner. It turned out that handkerchief belonged to Harry Stevens, one of Mrs. Hall's brothers. All three siblings—Willie Stevens, Henry Stevens, and Mrs. Frances Hall—were called in for questioning. A woman was asked to come into the room when Mrs. Hall was there. She stared at Mrs. Hall, nodded, and then left. No arrests were made.

The second break was that Mrs. Mills's daughter Charlotte found her mom's love letters and a diary in the crocheted bag behind the living room door. Instead of turning it over to the prosecutors though, Charlotte Mills (who now hired an attorney, Florence North) had her attorney sell the letters for $500 to the *New York American* magazine. She said "the prosecutors had not cooperated with her, so she saw no need to cooperate with them." (It later came out in court that it was her father, Jimmy Mills, who sold the letters and Charlotte was covering for him.)

The third break occurred on Wednesday, October 18, when a conclusive report about the blood found around the crab-apple tree came in from the chemist who had done a soil analysis. The chemist believed that because only 0.08 of a pint of blood was found in the soil, it was likely that Mrs. Mills's throat had been cut after she was dead, and it was unlikely that the victims had been killed elsewhere and brought to the spot. This report put the official jurisdiction of the case in Somerset County.

The fourth break was the biggest break of all—an alleged eyewitness to the murder who assigned blame to Mrs. Hall and her brothers. A fifty-year-old woman by the name of Jane Gibson stepped forward. She owned a sixty-acre pig farm near the Phillips farm. She became known as the "Pig Lady."

The Pig Lady claimed to have heard one of her dogs bark at 9:00 p.m. on September 14. She saw a shadowy figure pass by her front door, and then she heard a rickety old wagon go right through her cornfield. Thinking that it was the same corn thief who had stolen twenty rows of corn from her just the previous Sunday, she grabbed her rifle, mounted her shoeless mule Jenny (which made her a perfect silent stalker), and followed the "thief" into the cornfields with the intention of pumping some lead into him.

As she followed the wagon up De Russey's Lane onto Easton Avenue, an automobile had entered De Russey's Lane as well. The headlights of the car allowed her to catch a glimpse of a black man and white woman in the road. (The black man was later thought to be Willie Stevens, who was Caucasian but had a dark complexion and kinky black hair.) By then she lost sight of the wagon. She figured the corn thief might have cut back into the cornfield, so she took a shortcut and rode her mule until she came to a little path that led to the Phillips farm. She then got off her mule and tied him near "two little cedar trees and a stump."

It was then she heard loud arguing coming from the crab-apple tree. As she got closer she saw four figures silhouetted against the night sky. According to her story, as her eyes grew accustomed to the darkness, she realized it was two men and two women. She heard one woman scream, "Explain these letters."

Then a fight began, and people were struggling. She heard a shot and ran to her mule. She heard someone say, "Oh, Henry." She heard someone running, then someone being dragged, then a woman scream, "Don't, don't, don't!" She claimed to have heard three more shots as she was backing away on her mule. Then she saw a body falling to the ground. A few seconds later, she saw what she believed was a woman put her hand on a man's shoulder and say, "Oh, Henry." Then she rode away.

The Pig Lady said she went back around 1:00 a.m. to retrieve a moccasin she had lost while riding the mule. She said that the moon had just risen and when she got back to the crime scene she heard crying. Because the moon was bright, she was able to clearly see that it was Mrs. Hall crying by her dead husband's body. (Later a weather report verified that indeed on that night the moon had risen at 12:26 a.m.)

The Pig Lady's story had some inconsistencies, however. In the story she originally told authorities, there were three men and one woman who killed the victims—a total of six people. She later told reporters she saw a total of four people, and in that telling she described Willie Stevens's looks but claimed Mrs. Hall yelled out the name "Henry." She told the reporters she had told two different stories on purpose and then said, "And when I get on the stand, I will give you a better story yet."

When the press asked why she didn't come forward right away, she said that she wanted to stay out of it at first but when the Hayes boy got accused "she couldn't stand by and let an innocent boy take the rap." It was then that she went to the police, but no one would listen to her. (The police later verified the fact that she did attempt several times.) But finally someone did listen to her. The Pig Lady was the woman who had been brought in to look at Mrs. Hall when she was being questioned. Once she made a positive ID, the police wanted to investigate further.

With the Pig Lady's accusations and Eleanor's letters and Hall's diary going public, the five-week-old case now garnered renewed interest from the press. Over one hundred reporters from around the country were now assigned to the case. They gathered at the farm, and it now took on a carnival-like atmosphere, with vendors selling balloons and refreshments near the site of the murders.

To end political bickering over jurisdiction, Wilbur A. Mott of Essex County was appointed Deputy Attorney General in charge of the case by a New Jersey Supreme Court judge, who wanted the media circus to end and thought Mott would move the investigation forward. Mott got his star witness's testimony ready for trial. Many didn't believe Jane Gibson, the Pig Lady, because her story went from a two-page affidavit to a six-page account over time. Ms. Gibson explained that it was because she was being asked a lot more questions.

Forty-three days later, as the press and citizens were still lurking around the murder scene, two unexploded cartridges were found. For the first time since the murders, the crime area was closed off and state troopers conducted a complete search of the farm.

On Wednesday, November 8, Mott said, "Our case is complete." He was ready to ask for the indictments of Mrs. Hall, Mr. Willie Stevens, and Mr. Henry Stevens. Unfortunately for him however, the presiding judge had just finished a lengthy murder trial and was taking a vacation until November 19, which gave Mrs. Hall's attorney time to come up with a counter punch. He talked to a neighbor of the Pig Lady, a Mrs. Nellie Russell, who signed an affidavit claiming the Pig Lady was with her on the night of the murders, not out riding her mule as she had claimed. She said that the Pig Lady had found Mrs. Russell's lost dog and returned it to her that very night at 10:00 p.m. Mott had no intention of letting the grand jury call Russell as a witness, because at the moment Russell's story totally contradicted the Pig Lady's story. (Later it turned out that Mrs. Russell hated Gibson and also had her dates mixed up—her story was almost certainly a fabrication.)

By Saturday night, all of Mott's fifty subpoenas had been sent out. He told the press that "Everything was ready to be presented to the grand jury." He would not say, however, that he was confident about getting an indictment.

The trial began on November 20, 1922, at 9:30 a.m. The press was barred from the courtroom, although they gathered in droves outside the court building.

Witness after witness took the stand, from the couple who found the bodies, to the first reporter on the scene, to the police officers, to neighbors, to the Halls' housemaids, to churchgoers who heard gossip about the minister and the choir girl, to delivery boys, to the chemist with the bloody soil sample . . . everyone who had any tiny involvement with the case whatsoever.

It took five days and sixty-seven witnesses for the grand jury to reach their determination. With the announcement that the jury refused to indict, the Iron Widow, dressed in black, stood up, held her head high, and without emotion walked with her attorney and best friend to her car. The press ran to report the decision. The case now lost steam.

The case was dead for almost four years, until July 3, 1926. Arthur Riehl had married Mrs. Hall's ex-maid, Louise Geist. After he filed for divorce, he released a statement to the press that his ex-wife had been paid $5,000 by Mrs. Hall to keep quiet about what happened the night of the murders. Apparently Geist told Mrs. Hall that her husband was going to run off with Mrs. Mills. Mrs. Hall then had Peter Tumultry (her cousin Henry Carpender's chauffeur) drive her and her brother, Willie Stevens, to the Phillips Farm. Geist said Willie was a good shot and his pistol was kept in the Hall library drawer. Riehl's statement made the front page of the *New York Daily Mirror*. It sold hundreds of papers and the editor of the paper, Phil Payne, dared Governor A. Harry Moore to reopen the Hall-Mills case. Some said Payne did it to sell newspapers; he claimed he did it in the name of justice.

At 10:00 a.m. on July 28, 1926, the new prosecutor, Francis Bergen, called Justice William Sutphen and said he had "certain evidence" that pointed to Mrs. Hall as one of the murderers in the case. A warrant for her arrest was issued. By 3:00 a.m. she was arraigned and put in a holding cell.

This time the state prosecutors were keeping tight-lipped. Bergen said, "What botched the last trial was premature publication of evidence. We will make public nothing." A new special prosecutor had also been assigned to the case—a state senator from Hudson County, Alexander Simpson.

Simpson was appalled by the amount of evidence that seemed to have vanished or been tarnished since 1922. Missing was Willie Stevens's gun, witness statements, the autopsy reports, the reverend's shirt collar, and his cuff buttons. Hall's eyeglasses were tarnished, and they had been wiped clean of fingerprints. Simpson put detectives on the case to track down the missing evidence and find out what happened.

While evidence was being rounded up, Mrs. Hall had been released on bail and had hired a defense team of top attorneys with Robert H. McCarter as the lead counsel.

As the new trial approached, Jimmy Mills admitted he had seen his wife's letters, knew about his wife's affair all along, and would have divorced her if he had the money. His wife, Eleanor, knew that he knew because he complained to her about it, but she didn't seem to care. As for their daughter, Charlotte, she claimed that the prosecutor had coached her on what to say before the grand jury and told her, "There are certain places for girls of your kind when they don't know how to behave."

Simpson was busy all week. After getting fifty-seven statements from witnesses, he now secured two more warrants for arrests, that of Mrs. Hall's brother, Willie Stevens, and of her first cousin, the stockbroker, Henry Carpender. They were each charged with "the murder of each deceased."

On August 13, 1926, the new preliminary hearing with Simpson at the helm began with Judge Cleary on the bench. This hearing would determine if Simpson could establish a prima facie case to hold the trio for murder. Fifty-four witnesses were called to the stand.

Several pieces of vital new information came out in the hearing. Robert Erling, a local millwright and neighbor of Jane Gibson, aka the Pig Lady, claimed to have seen her on De Russey's Lane on her mule between the hours of 9:00 and 10:00 p.m. He too was "with a married woman" in the car at the time, and thus chose not to come forward. This statement added credibility to the Pig Lady's story.

Lieutenant Edward Schwartz, the fingerprint superintendent of Newark's Bureau of Records, had found unshod hoof marks of a mule near the cedar tree where Ms. Gibson said she tied up her mule. Schwartz had taken the photos of the footprints back in October of that year and had the film but never developed it. This statement added more credibility to the 1922 star witness who testified that the mule she took was without shoes and therefore perfect for stalking a corn thief.

After hearing all the testimony, Judge Cleary determined that the state had made a sufficient case to proceed forward to a grand jury for them to make a determination. Everyone except the Hall family was thrilled.

Then, while Simpson was getting things in order for the case, two more witnesses came forward: church vestryman Ralph Gorsline and choir member Catherine Rastall, who claimed they too were having an affair and had witnessed the murder, but had been afraid to come forward. According to their story Ralph had encountered a gun-toting Henry Stevens that night, who had cautioned him never to tell anyone about what he had witnessed.

It took the grand jury only ten minutes to come back with two indictments accusing Mrs. Hall, Willie Stevens, Henry Stevens, and Frances's cousin Henry Carpender for the double murders. After the jurors had left the courtroom, a jubilent Simpson asked for a bench warrant for the arrest of Henry Stevens. It was granted. Arraignments were made and the defendants all pleaded not guilty. Now, after four years, the trial would begin and that was a huge victory for the prosecution.

Wanting everything possible to be in the state's favor and to get a fair trial, Simpson requested a "foreign jury" (one outside the county that was not prejudiced to all that had happened in the preceding four years). His request was denied. But Simpson was granted "trials of severance," meaning two separate trials: one trial for Mrs. Hall and her two brothers, and a separate trial, at a later date, for her cousin, Henry Carpender. His request was accepted.

Just before the trial was to begin, Felix De Martini was arrested. De Martini was a private detective hired by Mrs. Hall in 1922 who worked with her attorney. The charge was for intimidating and influencing witnesses; he had apparently told Pig Lady Jane Gibson to "get out of town" at the time of the first grand jury trial.

The trial of Mrs. Hall and her two brothers was set for Wednesday, November 3, 1926. The Somerville courtroom could accommodate 275 spectators, and every seat was filled because over three hundred journalists from the U.S. and Europe had already come in to report on the case. Extra wire lines were set up to get the news out.

For three weeks Simpson brought witnesses in to build his case. In his prosecution he revealed that Willie's footprint was found at the scene of the murder, and also that his left index fingerprint was on the business card found at the scene of the crime.

Simpson had many supporting witnesses who added credence to the Pig Lady's story, though he had to fight to get Ms. Gibson to court. During the trial the Pig Lady was ill and hospitalized. Apparently, a doctor was being paid off to claim the Pig Lady was in no position to testify. But she desperately wanted to.

PHOTO COURTESY OF FRAN CAPO

The Somerset County Courthouse, where the famous Hall-Mills murder trial took place in 1926.

Simpson, with a great deal of effort, managed to sneak her out of the hospital and get her to court in her hospital bed, which in itself became quite a spectacle.

After seventeen days the prosecution rested its case.

It was now up to the defense team, who took turns speaking to the jury. Their opening statement said they were out to prove that all three defendants not only did not kill Eleanor Mills but were also nowhere near the Phillips Farm on the night of the murders. They ended by saying, "after you hear their stories, your conscience and minds will be free to acquit them."

Willie's only defense was that he was in his room until Mrs. Hall asked him to go to the church with him to find out if the minister had fallen asleep there. According to his testimony they went over to the church and when they didn't see Reverend Hall there, they decided to go to the Mills's house to see if he was there instead. When they stood outside the Mills's house they saw the lights were out, so they assumed he wasn't there and returned home. Willie's alibi was that one of their housemaids had said he was home.

Henry's alibi was a real fish story; he produced witnesses who said he had been fishing on the day in question, but they all wilted under cross-examination.

Fingerprint experts were brought in on both sides. The final determination was that it was indeed Willie's left index fingerprint on the business card, but that the card was not the original card at the scene. Mrs. Hall then gave the same story she had to the police earlier.

The defense brought in character witnesses to undermine the Pig Lady. They said that she was known as "a compulsive liar," and that she paid her neighbor $100 to say that he saw her on De Russey's Lane with her mule that night.

It had been exactly four weeks since the trial began, and it was time for the case to go to the jury. At 1:52 the jury of twelve farmers left the courtroom to deliberate. Thousands waited with bated breath. The courtroom emptied out as the hours went on. More than 170 people had testified, and 5,098 pages of testimony filled the records. The *New York Times* had devoted sixty-two pages of print to the case in 1922. In 1926, the trial was on the front page ninety times.

By 6:48 p.m. the jurors had reached a verdict. In minutes the courtroom was filled again. The foreman stood up and read the individual verdicts. Henry Stevens, Willie Stevens, and Mrs. Hall were all found not guilty.

Reporters surrounded the jurors. They said it took three ballots to come to the decision. In the end they said they just did not believe the Pig Lady's testimony. Further they felt there was too much bumbling of the initial investigation and evidence lost. After the acquittals all charges against all four were dropped.

So who was it? The rich Hall family, who could easily have paid off people to look the other way? The timid Jimmy Mills? A jealous choir singer? A crafty thief? The lying Ray Schneider?

A random crazy person? The Ku Klux Klan? Too much went wrong in this case from the start, with a destroyed crime scene, missing and contaminated evidence, political holdups, and witness tampering.

Today, De Russey's Lane is a huge street known as Franklin Boulevard, and where Phillips Farm sat is now a huge housing development.

The Hall-Mills murder is still considered an open case on the books of the Somerset County prosecutor. The common consensus among today's prosecutors is that the rich Hall family is responsible for the murders. Although no smoking gun was ever found, prosecutors believe that a semi-automatic handgun was used. The only people who could afford a semi-automatic gun at the time were the rich. The Hall family had the kind of money and connections to obtain that kind of gun, and the cousin, Henry Carpender, had the shooting ability to use it. Unfortunately, it's unlikely that this case will ever be considered solved, as almost all evidence has disappeared and all of the main players have passed away. It remains one of the greatest mysteries in New Jersey history.

CHAPTER 4

The Darker Side of Thomas Edison

There is an old Cherokee Indian story that says in each of us lurks two fighting wolves . . . one good, one bad. The bad wolf is filled with envy, greed, arrogance, false pride, superiority, and ego. The good wolf is filled with love, hope, serenity, humility, kindness, empathy, truth, compassion, and faith. The wolf that wins the fight is the one you feed.

Thomas Edison is known by many as a hero, and indeed he was, when you look at his life's accomplishments. He holds the world record for the most patents with 1,368. Among his patented inventions were the electrical vote recorder, automatic telegraph system, paraffin paper, universal stock ticker, electric pen, phonograph, incandescent lamp, wireless telegraphy, and special experiments relating to the defense of the United States. All his inventions were developed in the Garden State, first in his Menlo Park Laboratory, then at his West Orange factory. Many of his inventions made our lives easier and flung us into a new age of technology.

Edison had the same traits that are attributed to many leaders: strong-willed, competitive, determined, and relentless. He was known to be a hard taskmaster, and those who worked for him were required to produce inventions, no matter what the cost—reportedly even stealing ideas or patents from others.

Ironically, the inventions he is most noted for—like the lightbulb, telegraph, movie camera, power generator, storage battery (which made Edison the most money), and electric chair—were in fact not his inventions.

For example, Edison did not invent the lightbulb. Joseph Swan was installing them in people's homes and landmark buildings in England before Edison even got his lightbulb working. The lightbulb, in fact, existed fifty years prior to Edison. He patented it in 1879 but then lost the patent both in Britain and the United States. What he did do was develop the first commercially practical incandescent electric lamp. As for the movie camera, one of his employees, William Dickson, invented it. It was jumpstarted by Edward Muybridge, a British photographer, who took pictures of a horse galloping and placed them into fast action stills. Nor did Edison invent the first electrical power station, but he did improve on existing generators, making them commercially successful.

One of Edison's most famous and valued employees was Croatia-born inventor Nikola Tesla, who held over three hundred patents in his lifetime. It was Tesla, for example, not Edison, who invented the power generator in the early 1880s. In

1887, it was Tesla, not Edison, who was the first to investigate the nature of x-rays.

Tesla began working for Continental Edison in 1882 in Paris, France. He was hired to resolve some problems Edison was having with his DC dynamos. When Tesla moved to the United States in 1884, practically penniless, he worked for Edison yet again, this time to improve Edison's DC dynamos. Edison saw Tesla's genius and offered him $50,000 for the job. However, just a year later, Tesla quit working for Edison because Edison refused to pay Tesla the promised money for the improvements. When asked for his pay, Edison laughed and said, "It was just a joke." Tesla resigned in disgust and the feud between the men began.

But this was Edison's way. He was a far better businessman than inventor. His inventions were not major breakthroughs and he often took credit for the ideas of others. Most of his patents were improvements on existing products. He knew how to get his "inventions" patented first and bring them to the commercial market to monetize them. He is quoted as saying, "I always invent to obtain money to go on inventing."

Some argue that since some of the true inventors were employees of Edison, he had a right to claim the inventions as his. Others say he could have registered patents under his company name with the actual credit for the invention being shared by the true inventor and Edison.

But who was supposed to get the credit in this situation: Edison or Tesla? Edison was rich and famous. Tesla was broke

The desk of famed inventor Thomas Alva Edison, located in his
studio home in West Orange, New Jersey. Edison would often
work at his desk until he fell asleep.

PHOTO COURTESY OF FRAN CAPO

and miserable. Some say Tesla was a swindler who deceived
investors into giving him money for one invention, only to use
it first on another. Of course, there are two sides to every story.

But in the spirit of competition, sometimes our evil side
shines. Some people are determined to win, no matter the cost.
Such was the case with the battle of the electric chair, or more
specifically, the electric currents.

The year was 1882, and Edison had literally lit up the
commercial and financial district of New York City near Pearl
Street with his direct current (DC), thus launching the age of
electricity. Direct current required thick copper wires and power
stations set up close together. It was the invention of the day and

Edison's stock values were high. It was the only game in town and he had JP Morgan and John D. Rockefeller on his side. Edison was a happy inventor.

However, four years later, George Westinghouse used Nikola Tesla's invention to light up Buffalo, New York, with his alternating current (AC). The "War of the Currents" had begun.

Unfortunately for Edison, AC seemed to be the winner, since it could be transmitted over great distances for a low cost. Clients of Edison's DC started flocking to Westinghouse. The stock price of Edison's company dropped. Determined to win the battle of the currents, Edison set out to demonize AC. But how?

Luckily for Edison, in 1886 the legislature had formed a "commission to investigate and report to the legislature the most humane and approved method of carrying into effect the sentence in capital cases." In other words, they needed to find a more humane way of executing people than hanging.

Edison appeared before the execution commission and convinced the commissioners that death by electricity, by AC electricity, would be quick and painless. This sparked an idea in Edison . . . literally. He was so determined to prove that AC was a "killer current" that he decided to launch a publicity campaign with executed animals as his proof. So in 1887, he wrote to the local ASPCA asking for "good sized cats and dogs."

He then hooked up dozens of cats and dogs with 1,000 volts of DC current, showing a dog could be hurt, but live. Then he would shock the same animal with 800 volts of AC current and kill the dog. He did this experiment thousands of times using innocent animals of all sizes. He invited the press to observe the experiments and they described these proceedings in detail. The term "electrocution" was coined to describe execution by electricity. The humane execution debate continued for a few years, with lethal injection as one choice being tossed aside because of opposition by doctors.

On June 4, 1888, New York State legalized death by electricity. That same month, an inventor by the name of Harold Pitney Brown wrote an editorial in the *New York Post* talking about a tragic accident that left a young boy dead when he touched an exposed telegraph that used AC current. In his editorial he accused "AC manufacturers and distributors of putting their own financial interests ahead of public welfare." He suggested that AC current be limited to 300 volts. Of course, Westinghouse rebutted and said it was safer than DC because it entered people's homes at a lower voltage.

This was perfect fodder for Edison. One month later, in July of 1888, Edison hired Harold P. Brown to do experiments in his West Orange lab. Brown and his assistant, Dr. Fred Peterson, designed an electric chair just so Edison could discredit Tesla's AC current. He wanted AC current to be associated with electrocutions. Edison's lab then became an execution chamber for thousands of animals.

On July 30, 1888, Brown and an assistant administered a series of DC shocks to a large Newfoundland mix dog. First they gave him 1,000 DC volts, putting the dog in agony, but not killing it. Then the dog was killed with a second charge of 330 volts of AC current. Edison ordered follow-up demonstrations but the ASPCA found out about it and interceded on behalf of the next dog to be electrocuted. (It was killed later at another demonstration.)

The ASPCA stopped supplying animals to Edison. But Edison was hell-bent on proving his point, so he purchased stray cats and dogs from local schoolboys for 25 cents each.

Edison set up public executions for the press, starting small with dogs and cats, but moving on to bigger and bigger animals, as he felt the need to prove his point. It wasn't long before he approved the death of sheep, an orangutan (whose hair caught on fire), cows, horses, and then the motherlode of them all, a pachyderm. How did he come across an elephant? Topsy, a circus elephant in Coney Island's Luna Park, had assaulted a patron. (In the elephant's defense, the patron had fed the elephant a lit cigarette, so naturally she attacked.) But nonetheless, the elephant's owner decided to kill the three-ton beast. Edison saw a newspaper story about Topsy and jumped at the chance. He offered to wire the elephant with AC current, and film it for the world to see.

Execution day came for Topsy, and when the switch was turned, the poor elephant was jolted to stiffness, smoldered a bit, then within ten seconds lurched forward and died. The press reported, "Alternating current will undoubtedly drive the hangman out of business." Yet despite the trail of animal deaths, people favored AC current. This infuriated Edison.

Edison, never one to give up, decided he had to prove his point on none other than the ultimate target—man. With Brown and Edison working together, they convinced the superintendent of prisons to let them supply the electrocution apparatus—an electric chair wired with Westinghouse's AC current. The committee agreed. But Westinghouse refused to sell his generators directly to the New York State Prison authorities.

Edison did some smooth talking behind the scenes and was able to get a competitor of Westinghouse, the Thomson Houston Electric Company, to smuggle in three second-hand Westinghouse generators through a dealer in Boston into the Auburn prison in New York. They paid $7,000 for the generators. The next day, on May 13, 1889, William Kemmler (aka John Hart), "a brute who chopped a woman to bits with an axe," was sentenced to death by electrocution. He would be the first person to die "humanely" through the electric chair. This story made headlines.

Westinghouse hired lawyers to defend Kemmler and appealed to New York State that electrocution was cruel and unusual punishment. A hearing was held and Edison and Brown, who both claimed to be against capital punishment, assured the court that in their expert opinion, AC current was quick and painless. When asked if they were using this argument because they had a financial interest in the success of DC current, they both denied it, saying they were doing it in the name of humanity. The courts dismissed Westinghouse's objections and the execution was to take place as scheduled. Westinghouse did not want the deaths associated with his voltage. But it was too late; the AC generators were already in place, and the electric chair had been wired with AC current without Westinghouse's knowledge. At 6:00 a.m. on August 6, 1890, Kemmler entered the death chamber in the basement of the administration building of the prison. The agent and warden and twenty-five official witnesses (fourteen of whom were doctors) were in attendance and were seated in a semicircle. The prisoner was introduced to the witnesses. He was calm. When signaled by the warden, he removed his coat and took a seat in the square-framed heavy oaken electric chair. A leather mask was put on his head so the witnesses could not see his eyes popping out.

Kemmler asked the guards to "take their time and do it right." It took all of ten minutes for the switch, releasing 1,300 volts of alternating current, to be released. The first jolt lasted seventeen seconds and had to stop because one of the belts on the generator was about to come off. At first it appeared Kemmler was dead, as he remained lifeless for a half a minute, still smoldering and bleeding. But then they realized he wasn't dead and a second jolt of AC current was administered for seventy seconds. For four minutes the smell of burning flesh filled the room, while the burnt body bobbed up and down in the chair. Finally Kemmler was pronounced dead at 6:49 a.m. The execution took eight minutes.

To really drive home the point, and to try to strike the final blow in the battle, Edison supposedly bribed a journalist. The headline the next day read, KEMMLER WESTINGHOUSED. When asked for a rebuttal to the headline, Westinghouse had this to say: "They could have done it better with an axe." Despite all Edison's efforts, the DC current still lost out to AC, and some Edison products that relied on DC current had to be abandoned. Alternating current lights are in most of the homes in the United States today. In the end, the electrocution wasn't really about providing a humane way to electrocute people, but rather a way for one electric company to discredit another. Years later, Edison admitted that AC technology was superior to DC and that he knew it all along. It was just a game.

Perhaps if this darker side of Thomas Edison's career were more widely known, he would not be so revered in history text-books, and New Jersey would have towns and buildings named for Nikola Tesla.

CHAPTER 5

The Devil's Bathtub

There are many legends surrounding the Pinelands (or Pine Barrens, as the area is also known) of New Jersey. Some say packs of wild dogs roam the area, attack travelers, and drag them into the woods to be devoured, while others say it's mobsters' favorite hiding spot for dismembered and discarded bodies. The most famous legend, of course, is that of the New Jersey Devil. But what devil would just live in the woods and not have a really good place to hide or attend to hygiene? Enter the Blue Hole, a bottomless water pit in the woods known as "the Jersey Devil's bathtub" and a direct passageway to hell. It's a place where swimmers who dared to go into the mysterious waters later insisted they felt a hand come up from below and grab their legs, as they desperately tried to escape from becoming a morsel for the Devil. Tales of unexplained whirlpools that suck down unsuspecting swimmers are also part of the lore. Many who have survived the hole claim they felt themselves being pulled down, and that it took every ounce of their strength to come back up. Those who dared to go there at night claimed to have heard the hoof beats of the Devil as he raced through the woods and dove into his hideaway.

Legend has it that many have died in this mysterious hole. Is this the result of overactive imaginations, or is there some truth to the legend? As far back as 1837, people, especially kids, had been warned to stay away from the Blue Hole. The hole was rumored to be bottomless, and legend had it that the Jersey Devil loved to steal children, hurt them, and drag them down into oblivion. Old Joe Dixon, who was known as the hermit of the Blue Hole, used to warn the local boys to stay away from the mystery pool, just as he warned his own grandchildren to stay away.

In the 1930s it was a popular swimming hangout and was easily accessible. The Williamstown Volunteer Fire Company used to hold annual cookouts there.

A wooden footbridge over the Great Egg Harbor River was the way to get there, since the hole was situated just a tad south of the bridge. But the pathway to the hole was established long before the fire department started having cookouts. It was the same trail that the Lenape Indian tribe used to cross the Egg Harbor River.

The convenient footbridge was wiped out during a nasty hurricane in 1938. A new bridge was built just after the war with steel beams and wood planking, but the bridge was stolen plank by plank and beam by beam by enterprising thieves. By 1954, the last steel beam was gone, making it even more forbidding.

The locals call the area "Inskips." Story has it that so many rumors were going around about the hole that one day, John "Inskips" Brown, a very heavyset man, had enough talk of this scary blue hole and decided to check it out himself. He swam out to the middle of the hole and let out a shout. Everyone thought he was fooling around. But then he went down under, first once, then twice. When he went down a third time, onlookers went in with a boat and fished him out. They rolled the man around, and he came back to life. He said, "The Devil reached up and got me from deep in the pool." This story only made the legend grow bigger, and more people became afraid of the hole. Eventually, it was abandoned as a place for cookouts.

As if that wasn't enough, the area surrounding the Blue Hole had unstable sand, like many other parts of the Pine Barrens. If you dared to drive there, it was very easy to get your car stuck as it sank into the quicksand. There used to be warning signs posted everywhere not to swim, hunt, or light fires. But the signs only made those daredevil souls want to dare the Devil more. Often, they would do all three.

As with all good legends, there are groups that want to disprove the legend of the Blue Hole. In 1937 a group of scientists armed with a long line of cable and a huge weight took a boat into the middle of the hole and dropped a weight to test whether the pit was truly bottomless. Down, down, down the cable kept going until it was all fed out. They dropped more lines, and the same things happened. They could not reach a bottom in the center of the hole. With the scientists having verified the legend, the story of the bottomless pit was put into print in 1937 in a book entitled *More Forgotten Towns of Southern New Jersey*. The author was a South Jersey historian by the name of Henry Charlton Beck. Again the legend was thrust into the public eye.

People speculated about how the Blue Hole was formed. Some say it was formed by a prehistoric meteorite that raced to earth, gouged out a hole, and created an impact crater that filled with water. If you look at the shape of the hole you can see how that theory can apply, because it's almost perfectly circular and the edges come up as if formed by an impact. The depth of the hole around the sides is only about two feet, but then suddenly drops off into a steep shelf, which is consistent with the meteorite theory.

Others say that it is a pinto, a term geologists use to describe a small body of water that is the result of an ice mass that formed beneath permanently frozen solid ground during the Ice Age. The ice stayed this way for thousands of years, then at some point it broke through the permafrost and created a depression near a hill. When the climate warmed up in the area, the ice melted and formed a crystal pool of water. The die-hard legend seekers, however, want to believe it is a unique hole, with the sole purpose of being the bathtub for the Jersey Devil.

The only problem with all these theories, according to natural historian Mark Demitroff, is that the Blue Hole is not unique. Supposedly there are other similar holes in Newtonville and Egg Harbor Township, although no other legends surfaced

PHOTO COURTESY OF D. V. KILIAN

The "bottomless" Blue Hole, also known as the New Jersey
Devil's bathtub. The hole is located in the thick bush of the
Pine Barrens, near Egg Harbor River.

during the research for this book. Although Demitroff states that
"the science of blue holes is unique to the Pine Barrens," a quick
Google search shows blue holes elsewhere in the world, with the
deepest blue hole—Dean's Blue Hole in the Bahamas—having
a depth of 663 feet. By definition, those blue holes are vertical
caves or sinkholes.

Demitroff also states that "blue holes are places in or near
streams where large amounts of water under pressure well up and
shoot up like a geyser. They're large springs." That explains their
clear color, as opposed to nearby ponds and lakes.

Why is the Blue Hole blue? The bacteria in the brown water typical of ponds in the area come from the iron taken out of marl, a type of heavy soil. Add the temperature of the warmer lakes and ponds and it's the perfect breeding ground for bacteria, which along with tannic acid create the brown color. But the water in the blue holes comes from so far below the ground that the bacteria in the water are not active and therefore can't turn the water brown. It stays clear and glassy and reflects the color of the blue sky, hence the illusion of a blue hole. That deep water could also explain why there are whirlpool actions in the hole: since it may feed from ground water, surges of current could happen, creating the devilish whirlpool action.

Oddly, this Blue Hole still seems to hold its air of mystery and continues to attract curiosity seekers. A crew from a local newspaper journeyed there on January 19, 2009. While all other bodies of water were frozen, the Blue Hole had no ice on it. There was also odd vegetation growing in the water. They took a measuring rod and in some spots it was only seven feet deep. But the center of the hole where the water drops off was still "bottomless."

So what exactly is fact and what is fiction about this hole which is sometimes called by its other name: "the bottomless pit of Beelzebub"? A hole that is said to be surrounded in eerie silence, with no birds singing, no fish, no insects, nothing . . . just a creepy stillness? A hole that is said to have unusually large animal tracks found around the area with trees stripped of their bark very high up, which many claim are the claw marks of the Jersey Devil? A hole where it is said many bones of animals have been found imbedded in the sand at the edge?

Here's what is known to be fact: The Blue Hole is a clear, circular blue body of water about 120 feet in diameter with a deep shoreline, situated in the middle of the Pinelands, a sparsely populated, wooded area consisting of 1.1 million acres of land that contain many unusual plant species and animal life unique to the area. Tall pine trees circle the entire hole so it rarely gets more than two hours of sunlight a day.

Reports say that the water is usually bitterly cold with temperatures staying at a constant 40 to 50 degrees Fahrenheit, while all the other waters around it in the summer months are much warmer.

The hole itself is located in Monroe in Winslow Township, in Gloucester County off of Piney Hollow Road. If you decide you want to visit, you can do so by several methods. However, take caution: The road is very isolated and there probably will be traces of the satanic rituals that have been reported to take place there. It's located on state land, at the edge of the township.

Since the bridge has long been destroyed, it can only be reached by traipsing through the heavily wooded, swampy Pine Barrens on foot. If you come in from the "wrong" side, you will have to cross a very cold, deceptively swift river with a three-foot trench and silt at the bottom. There is an easier way to get to the Blue Hole, although the actual road itself is not easy to find. Try inputting the GPS coordinates of 838 Piney Hollow Road to get close to the easier access.

Two older gentlemen, Joe Gionti and Bob Ormsby, who are township natives and members of the township's historical society, are trying to keep the legend alive. Detailed maps to the Blue Hole are now available at the Ireland Hofer House Museum on Main Street in Williamstown. Signs now mark the spot that has been hard to get to for the past forty years.

> The coordinates of the Blue Hole:
> N 39 deg 37.589'
> W 74 deg 53.734'
> Or more precisely:
> 39°37'35"N 74°53'45"W

But take heed: There is quicksand-like mud on the path, or maybe that's just the trickster Devil having a good laugh as he tries to draw you into his lair.

CHAPTER 6

The Insane Ghosts of Overbrook Asylum

hen it was built in 1896 it was beautiful: 325 acres dotted with sixty Victorian buildings sitting on sprawling green land at 150 Fairview Avenue in the area then known as Verona (now known as Cedar Grove).

This beautiful facility was not built as some fancy vacation resort or spa. Instead, the Essex County Board of Chosen Freeholders decided to build an upscale, state-of-the-art facility to house patients with all types of severe mental illnesses, people whose mental illnesses disabled them so much they could not function without supervised care. In other words . . . the insane.

The complex of buildings sat on the bottom of the hill on a large parcel of land right there for New Jersey taxpayers to see. It was originally called the Essex County Asylum for the Insane. It later took on the local shorthand name of Overbrook, since it was over the tiny Peckman River, which locals thought of as a brook. To confuse things even further, it later became known as the Essex County Mental Hospital. (This was often confused with the Essex

Mountain Sanatorium, which was located on the same property and housed tuberculosis patients.)

Now needless to say people in the neighborhood were not thrilled with a bunch of "crazies" being right next to them, especially when many of them would casually drift off the property and show up in nearby backyards. In one instance a patient walked off in his pajamas, broke into a home, forced a Cedar Grove housewife into her car at knifepoint, and drove off. He was later arrested in Pennsylvania and returned to the institution, but these incidents were not rare. They happened throughout the entire history of the insane asylum. There were over 150 missing patients in 1978 alone!

When the insane asylum first opened, caregivers had no choice but to lock up the patients and keep them quiet, relaxed, and away from the general population. Back then there were no "wonder drugs" for the treatment of various brain disorders. The hope was that one day they could return to mainstream society, but in reality most patients had a one-way ticket. In its heyday over three thousand patients were housed at Overbrook.

Because there were so many people on the property to take care of, the facility managers did the only logical thing they could: They became a town within a town so they could become self-sufficient.

In order to feed the masses, they grew their own crops on the land that was maintained by both the nearby Essex County Jail inmates and the in-house patients. This served a dual purpose: Not only did they not have to buy food from an outside source, but at the same time it was "therapy." For the inmates, the farm allowed them to do an honest day's work and help pay their dues to society. For the patients, it became part of their occupational therapy.

In addition to crops, there were also livestock: a herd of cows to supply milk for the asylum. Overseeing an operation like this took professional assistance. So the asylum employed a farmer to manage it all for a substantial salary plus free living space; he lived in a $50,000 home, which was quite palatial by the standards of the time.

But it didn't end there. The facility had three working wells that pumped 300,000 gallons of water per day from aquifers 600 feet below the surface to all the buildings. In addition, they had their own bakery, firehouse, butcher shop, Laundromats, and theater. For sports enthusiasts, they had their own semiprofessional baseball team. Overbrook even had a train stop designated just for them on the Erie Railroad. After all, they also needed a way to bring in massive amounts of coal to furnish steam for heating and power.

Despite all its outside beauty, the place still had a feeling of eeriness about it, partly because of the type of residents, but also because of what occurred behind those walls. Many types of restraints were used to keep the patients under control, as they often became increasingly desperate to escape once confined.

And if mental illness wasn't enough to give visitors goosebumps, there were more than a few tragedies that occurred at

Overbrook. In the winter of 1917, the boiler failed and as a result, twenty people froze to death overnight in their beds. The *New York Times* reported: "The 1,800 insane patients at the Essex County Hospital, at Cedar Grove, NJ, are suffering serious discomfort and in some cases incurring danger from the practically complete collapse of the heating and lighting plant of the institution. The sleeping quarters of the inmates are practically without heat, and have been so during the recent cold snap . . . the management of the institution has even been trying to borrow a locomotive from one of the railroads to furnish steam for heating and power." During that tragedy alone twenty-four patients died in twenty days. Thirty-two other residents suffered from frostbite. When things like this happen, death lingers in the air. But this was only the beginning of the thousands of deaths that these buildings would bear witness to.

During the Great Depression, many of the buildings at Overbrook became a refuge for the hungry, homeless, and destitute population. It was a lot to handle. In addition, veterans of World War II with no place to turn were integrated into the mix. With food being rationed and the addition of both the homeless and the soldiers suffering from post-traumatic stress disorder, the hospital was overrun and could not care for all of its patients. The patients who came there for refuge suffered from abuse, neglect, and dismal conditions at the hospital, which only compounded the situation.

The veterans who were hoping to find a place to heal instead were faced with violence among the residents, coupled with starvation, neglect, and abuse. They had nowhere else to go. Many of the mentally ill patients escaped using the underground tunnel systems. Some were captured and then punished brutally for their attempts. Others just committed suicide.

The staff tried to maintain order as best they knew how. But, due to being overworked and desperate, they resorted to many barbaric treatments of the day: pre-frontal lobotomies, diathermy, and hydrotherapy.

Stories started to surface about the dire situation at Overbrook. People in town would sometimes take a shortcut through the property to get to their homes. They would report patients hanging out the windows screaming at the top of their lungs. If they drove by at night, patients were literally howling at the moon.

However, things began to change in the 1960s, with the advent of new medicines. Fewer mentally ill patients needed to be sent to the asylum, which made it more manageable, and the institute's population slowly abated. With fewer people, many of the buildings became abandoned. Overbrook continued to operate, but the damage due to the long period of overpopulation was already done.

In total, over ten thousand patients died at Overbrook. In 2007 the hospital closed its doors for the last time due to the effects of many decades of much-deserved bad publicity. Essex County announced that a more modern institute would be built in Newark and all patients transferred there.

But not all of the patients went.

With so much death and suffering, the place became a prime setting for the ghosts of unhappy patients who decided their passing was not complete and chose to hang around eternally in their prison, even if the physical buildings were no longer there. Most of Overbrook's buildings were set to be demolished, but as with most large-scale projects, things take time. The buildings that were scheduled for demolition did not come down immediately and sat empty for many years. The site became a favorite hangout for teens looking for adventure. Stories of ghost sightings spread and it almost became a rite of passage for teenagers to venture into the abandoned buildings to see if they could come face to face with the tortured souls.

As the stories and sightings grew, so did the number of curiosity seekers. Soon it became necessary for the sheriff to post a notice warning that trespassers would be prosecuted. The Sheriff's Department stayed true to their word. From Friday, July 18, 2008, to Wednesday, July 29, 2008, a total of thirty-four arrests were made by plainclothes police officers. All the arrestees, both juveniles and adults ranging in age from sixteen to twenty, were detained at the Cedar Grove municipal jail. Summonses were issued to all the thrill seekers and all were charged with criminal trespass or criminal mischief. The police officers claimed they were merely trying to protect the intruders from the unseen dangers in abandoned buildings, including asbestos in the walls.

So what exactly did those eyewitnesses see or encounter that made them willing to risk arrest, or breakage of bodily limbs? On the outside, an observer would see overgrown grass, ivy-covered walls, graffiti, and each building labeled by number.

Those who ventured inside saw a mass of debris—evidence of neglect juxtaposed with glimmers of brightness. They saw scattered paper files, peeled walls, broken windows, overturned wheelchairs, murals, a list of meals and snacks on the wall, instructions on how to groom and dress, instructions on proper hygiene, and instructions on how to relax in a place jammed with people. Broken television sets lay scattered on the floor. Half-sheeted stained beds with the patients' names still stuck to them with masking tape were found next to bright posters about sharing. Heavy wooden doors labeled "sick rooms" abounded. Gated staircases were everywhere so no one could escape and order could be kept. The long hallways with open doors on rusty hinges were dark and foreboding, with negative energy oozing out of the doors as if they were portals to an unseen world. Some trespassers claim they heard people yell, "You'll burn in hell!" in those tunnels, and when they turned to see who had yelled out, no one was there.

The miles of underground tunnels were the most eerie. These tunnels connected all the buildings in the complex. They were dark, long passageways with peeled paint chips and exposed pipes and light fixtures overhead. The tunnels were the heart of the hospital, supplying water, heat, and electricity.

While the fifty buildings were still in use, people could access them through the ten abandoned buildings. The shared basements were filled with overturned desks, broken syringes, and other medical equipment that lay scattered on the floor. Discarded patients' shoes lay next to a dentist chair. Signs were posted everywhere, one stating, BUILDING CLOSED BY ORDER OF BOARD OF HEALTH.

Some of the buildings had wards and activity centers. Others were houses for the resident doctors, occupational buildings, or greenhouses. In one building there was a mural of the death tree (perhaps a patient's artwork) with black all around the tree and dangling skeletons on it. Next to it, a sign that read, SOBRIETY IS AN UPHILL JOURNEY. In the morgue were opened slab drawers with unfilled medical notes lying around that read, "I hereby certify that I made an examination of the body of _____ now lying dead at _____ facts concerning the circumstances of the death and the cause of the death are as follows: _____." Everyone who entered said the same thing. It felt creepy; they felt heaviness in the air as if the torture just hung there.

As the buildings were abandoned, county officials warned people again and again to stay out, but no matter how many arrests were made it was not deterring the morbidly curious from sneaking into the buildings. So the facility owners applied the theory, if you can't beat them join them!

If people were going to go in anyway, they might as well make money on it. So they started charging paranormal and ghost hunting groups the tidy sum of $1,000 per day to go in and look around, a nice way to bring in revenue for the county.

Eventually as with all legendary places, it became a target of the media. Television shows, such as *Extreme Ghost Adventures* on the Travel Channel, got permission to investigate the site. Local papers like the *Newark Star-Ledger* did stories on it as well.

Then Hollywood got involved. The setting was so eerie that director Clark Gregg, who adapted the novel *Choke* for his 2008 Australian movie of the same name, decided to use the abandoned mental hospital as the set. At the time of shooting, all but five buildings were gone, and they were all abandoned. The director was pleased with the location, although he wound up getting a lot more than he bargained for. As he put it, "We had three very tough guy cops who were there training police dogs while we were shooting, and they were so matter of fact that there were two different ghosts in two different buildings." Apparently one ghost was a sexy Florence Nightingale type, while the other ghost was far less friendly. One of Gregg's crew members walked into the fifth building to set up a shot. Afterward, he came out visibly shaken and said he had experienced an "unspeakable satanic dark energy." The crew member, whose name has been withheld, said it was so horrible that he refuses to talk about it even to this day for fear of conjuring up the entity's negative forces.

But that didn't deter other mediums from wanting to do their take on it. On April 29, 2009, the Syfy Channel rented the abandoned mental ward for their show titled *Ghost Hunters*. They taped an episode called "The Garden State Asylum" because they didn't want to disclose the real name or their exact location. According to *Ghost Hunters*, "Most ghostly activities took place in building number 11, the building that was used as both the morgue and to house the criminally insane." The people from the show heard screams, loud banging, and verbal threats to get off the property.

A few months later, on July 1, 2009, demolition began at Overbrook. Joe Divincenzo Jr., the county executive, was at the control of the bulldozer as city officials and press watched. The bulldozer's metal claws ripped into the windows and clawed their way down taking the brick walls with it.

As for the land, the plans were simple. Originally, the entire Overbrook property was going to be developed for upscale housing. It was sold at a very low price to the developers, who in turn were going to get a very high price for their houses. But that plan fell apart in January 2009, thanks to Divincenzo Jr., who wanted a state park to be built on some of the land. Because of his bargaining, only the western side of Fairview Avenue became privately owned upscale housing. A sign on the eastern side reads, FUTURE SITE OF 90 ACRES OF PASSIVE PARKLAND. One can't help but wonder if the spirits will hang around there to haunt the park visitors as they enjoy a family picnic.

CHAPTER 7

Housewives of Essex County

Mary Wilson had decided to go for a long walk along the ridge near the Montclair Hotel to clear her mind. She and her best friend and neighbor, Mrs. Edwin A. Preith, had a large problem they were trying to solve: a problem that affected their whole county, in fact their whole state.

As she walked along the ridge she looked out over the valley and saw the gorgeous colors of the evening sunset. She noticed the colors were bouncing off a glass object. As she looked longer she realized the colors were reflecting off the windows of the abandoned girls' home that sat on top of Orange Mountain, the highest point in Essex County. As she looked at the dazzling lights, a light in her own head went off. "That's it!" Her moment of inspiration had come and she knew she had the answer. She ran to tell her friend.

Mrs. Preith was ecstatic as well. They both knew that the home for wayward girls had quite a well-intentioned but sad history. It started innocently enough in 1873, as a way to help girls in need, but just seven short years later, a fire destroyed the Newark City Home for Girls. Although no one died in the fire, the idea of the single-building reform home for girls did. After the fire, the board of trustees for the Newark City Home for Girls, headed by Joseph Goetz, decided to expand the operation to a "cottage" system to house both boys and girls in clusters of fifty children per unit, making it more like an orphanage. The new building was opened in January 1902 on top of Orange Mountain (today known as Second Mountain), bordering both Verona and Caldwell in New Jersey.

The number of delinquent girls was too small for the cottage plan to work, and the home now stood vacant, alone on top of the hill—helping no one . . . and that's what these two housewives wanted to change. It was the year 1907, in the cold wintry month of February. They knew they were up against formidable odds: Women did not speak publicly at the time, much less in front of boards and political bodies, but they were determined and many lives were at stake. If they could convince people to listen to them, they could help not only the husband of the laundress that worked for Mrs. Preith, but all people who had tuberculosis. At last count, in 1906, 842 deaths from tuberculosis had occurred in the city of Newark alone and the toll was rapidly rising.

Originally, the only thing these women set out to do was help the laundress's husband by applying to the Board of Health for assistance. In doing so they were told they would have to make a disposition for his case. The two housewives went before Dr. Herman C. H. Herold, the president of the Board of Health, and pleaded their case. Herold was sympathetic, but told them his hands were tied. He told them that the board had to lie low because the city did not have the proper facilities to care for the many tuberculosis patients, and that the city was doing everything in their power to care for them using the existing facilities. The women left his office distraught but determined to come up with an answer, and in the meantime they also wanted to check out his story to see if it were true. Was the city helping these people at all?

They started to ask around and found one of the men the city was supposedly helping. This young father was dying slowly while living in the basement of a local restaurant. He was kept isolated in the basement without any money, and his only food source was the food that the kind restaurant owner would give him. His support from the Board of Health was nothing more than a Board of Health blanket. The housewives took it upon themselves to get the man into one of the two hospitals that did offer beds for pay for tuberculosis patients. They paid out of their own pockets. But there were three thousand other cases like this in the city. They swore to each other they would find a way to help these people; they just had to figure out where and how.

Meanwhile the women's appeal touched Herold. Shortly after at a meeting of the city council he summed up the situation. "I came here to tell you how inadequate are our accommodations for the care of tuberculosis patients, both indigents and those who can pay for their treatments. St. Michael's and the city hospital are the only two institutions in the city that receive tuberculosis patients. The home for crippled children takes bone tuberculosis patients, but will not take persons suffering from pulmonary tuberculosis. The question of caring for consumptives is being agitated all over the country, but we have had to lie low and say nothing because we have not adequate means for treating sufferers from the disease. . . . There were 842 deaths from tuberculosis in Newark last year . . . there is no doubt but that many of those who died in 1906 had been sick a number of years. There are now in the city at least three thousand cases of tuberculosis. Just how many there are it is impossible to state, because the disease is unreportable."

The women now felt they had found the answer. The abandoned city home had a heating plant and plenty of rooms, which were already equipped with beds and blankets. It was surrounded by six acres of land so they could keep the tuberculosis patients away from the general population. It was perfect, but they needed to be sure it was available.

They did some research and contacted Joseph Goetz, the trustee of the city home. He assured them that there was no legal obstruction to turning the girls' home into a tuberculosis sanatorium. The city already owned the building. He also told them that the location was also very desirable, and that "Caldwell is now considered to be next to Denver for beneficial results," meaning that its mountains, pure air, and water were considered equivalent to Colorado for the treatment of tuberculosis recovery. Armed with his assurance the women went back to the Board of Health to tell them their idea and what they thought was an easy solution.

Dr. Herold and Health Officer Chandler were on board from the start. They were authorized to go before the Common Council with the women's proposal. The women wanted to come so they could present the emotional and urgent call to action that they felt was necessary. This could have turned out to be a tactical error. The Common Council was all men. It was a boys' club and two women coming before them to speak on "men's business" was frowned upon as something they didn't want to encourage. But underneath their frilly dresses these were relentless women. Mrs. Preith mentioned that they had already cleared the legal issues with Mr. Goetz. Miss Wilson, who was the chief advocate for the cause, presented her case practically and logically, employing facts and figures, and both the council and the press were impressed. The February 20, 1907, evening edition of the *Newark News* reported the story and the press began following the progress of these women and their proposal.

Another edition of the paper followed up describing a Common Council meeting in which the City Council was asked to "prepare such resolutions, motions, ordinances or even legislative bills, as might be necessary to have approved, to transfer the building and fifteen acres of ground to the care and custody of the board of health and to permit the appropriation of funds for its maintenance as a sanatorium."

The women were thrilled. They had found a solution to help thousands and it was moving along rapidly. Papers were drawn up and Bill Number 384 was ready to go before the legislature. They appeared in the state capital of Trenton dressed in their finest clothes to lobby for the bill. Now they were really ruffling some feathers. The men told the ladies that such beautiful and charming women should be at home, that if they could trust them everything would be all right. They were scooted off and told that the men would handle it from there. The men did not want the women lobbying. The Nineteenth Amendment, which allowed women the right to vote, had not been passed yet. So the ladies reluctantly went home, leaving their bill in the hands of the men who supposedly knew how to handle such things.

They anxiously awaited news of their bill. Weeks went by and they heard nothing. Finally the anticipation was too much and they could wait no longer. When it was one week before the adjournment of the legislature, the women went to the Board of Health to inquire what had happened to the bill. To their disgust and shock they were told, "Oh, that—it's dead."

There's an old saying, "Hell hath no fury like a woman scorned." Multiply that by two: two women who knew that thousands of people were depending on that bill to be passed. They devised a plan to talk to every single assemblyman in Trenton, and they did!

As the *Morning Star* paper reported, "Whenever a member of the committee on municipal corporations showed himself, he was cornered by a pretty little figure in a gray tailored suit and a gray toque, from which streamed a long blue ostrich plume or a large-eyed pleader dressed all in black. The young women learned something of politics and they learned that they must not vary their appearance too much or they might be forgotten. They adopted a campaign uniform and stuck to it."

But it was a battle; the word was out for the boys' club to "kill the bill." Eventually sugar won over vinegar, and the bill came before the house. It lost by one vote. But this did not stop the women. They were more determined than ever because they knew they were close: They had the energy, the persistence, and they knew it was the right thing to do.

It also didn't hurt that the press these housewives were getting helped them win friends in high places. Senator Frelinghuysen helped convince the entire Senate to back the women's plan. The bill was passed unanimously at midnight. Mrs. Preith personally carried the bill to Governor Stokes's office. The pen Stokes used to sign the bill into action was sent as a gift to Miss Wilson, since she had been called away at the midnight hour to deal with a personal family illness and could not attend the signing.

On April 15, 1907, the *Morning Star* headlines read, TWO FRAIL WOMEN ROUT FIVE HUNDRED WISE MEN BY HARD WORK—THEY GET VERONA SANATORIUM BILL THROUGH. When asked about their long battle to get this bill through, Mrs. Preith was quoted as saying,

I'm very, very tired, but I'm very glad that we have won. I haven't found lobbying very pleasant, but all the officials have treated us courteously. I don't think it adds to one's popularity to do this kind of work. You see, it isn't possible to please everybody and some of my friends don't recognize me when they pass since I began to work for this bill. It's all over and the poor consumptives are to have proper care and treatment—that is, some of them are. This is the beginning of a great crusade in which all cities must one day join.

With that done, the two women withdrew from the public eye and went back to their daily lives. They accomplished their mission of getting the Essex Mountain Sanatorium opened. Mrs. Preith actually left Montclair, and Miss Wilson (now Mrs. Travis) did some community work for her husband's parish, always keeping a watchful but distant eye on the development of their heartfelt project.

Of course now that the bill had passed, it took on legs of its own. The president of the Board of Health and Health Officer Chandler, who were with the ladies from the start, now had their hands untied and were able to help those in the community. They wasted no time and set out to find a doctor to be the superintendent of the sanatorium. Dr. Edward Gluckman was chosen because he had recently completed studying and practicing treating tuberculosis patients. He was excited and ready to move forward as was the Board of Health.

The hard part was over now . . . or was it?

The board of trustees that so gladly told the women that there was no problem in handing over the girls' home to change into a sanatorium now had a slight change of heart. The Board of Health was told that the trustees "wished to retain their right to resume control at any time of the buildings." This did not sit well with the Board of Health. They were not going to let this opportunity that the women had fought so hard for slip through their fingers. They were not going to let the thousands waiting for care down. They continued to get the building ready for the patients despite the opposition of the board of trustees. The trustees got wind that the Board of Health was still moving forward without agreeing to their demands, so they decided to leak the news to the community, knowing that the citizens of Verona and Caldwell with fear in their hearts would ask for an injunction to stop the masses of tuberculosis patients from moving in. Massive citizen protests ensued.

The Board of Health had to do something fast before the injunction was sought. In the middle of the night in November 1907, they had the superintendent sneak several patients into the building. Once the patients were in, the citizens knew that to evict the good doctor and his patients court proceedings would have to take place. The citizens dropped the injunction knowing how horrible and heartless it would look to try to get these patients out once they were in. The die was cast.

The building became the Essex County Sanatorium in the City of Newark and on January 21, 1908, the sanatorium received the first two official patients of the 129 that were treated that first year. Funds of $15,000 were allocated to them for the first quarter. At the end, all that remained was $1.89.

Dr. Gluckman continued not only to be a spearhead, but a huge anti-tuberculosis fighter. The hospital was dedicated to "curable and incipient cases of consumption." The chronic and terminal cases were sent to the County Isolation Hospital. But even with only handling those "curable" cases, there wasn't enough room for the hordes of people coming in, and large numbers of patients started to be neglected.

It took another two full years before the county responded and considered tuberculosis to be a countywide problem. And it wasn't until 1917, another seven years later, that the Newark Board of Health strongly suggested that the county fulfill its obligation to the people and provide for the 4,012 citizens suffering from tuberculosis in Essex County's twenty-one communities. In order to meet the increased needs, they would have to enlarge the facility. Finally, an appropriation was made to build two more pavilions.

A board of managers, consisting of three freeholders and two physicians, was brought on board. Temporary shacks were erected to handle the immediate problem of overcrowding. The construction of eleven new buildings to accommodate the patients started in 1917 and all were completed and opened to patients by 1922.

When the Nineteenth Amendment was ratified on August 26, 1920, two more women (Mrs. Elisabeth Harris of Glen Ridge and Mrs. Edith Hyde Colby) became major players in the Essex County Mountain Sanatorium's future by adding the largest building to the site, the hospital building, and the Community Building, which housed an auditorium and a chapel. The women had a local artist draw a huge mural to liven up the place and give the patients a more aesthetically pleasing place to heal.

The word spread about this fantastic facility, and it wound up facing another problem. It became not only the treatment center for tuberculosis patients, but also the landing place for World War I vets who had suffered from lung injuries during the war, homeless children, and drug abusers. All could benefit from the clean air and pure mountain water.

Over the years, the facility grew in size and went from the original six acres to two hundred acres. In the process it often got confused with the famed Overbrook Mental Asylum, which was on the same plot of land but only at the bottom of the hill. The reason for the confusion was in some instances, when beds opened up in the sanatorium, mental patients from Overbrook were sent there. Add to that the fact that underground tunnels connected both facilities, the sanatorium at the top of the hill and the mental hospital at the bottom of the hill, and that the facilities shared the same farmland to feed the masses of patients. But each was a distinct building with a distinct purpose.

In the 1950s, with the discovery of Streptomycin, an anti-biotic drug that essentially cured TB, the tuberculosis epidemic subsided, and there were fewer patients. The buildings no longer needed to be in use and slowly became abandoned. For the time it was opened, it was considered a state-of-the-art facility, and during its operation it had a 50 percent recovery rate for tuberculosis. It was known as one of the finest treatment centers in the world.

In 1977 the last patient was released from the sanatorium. The doors were officially closed and the gates were locked on December 1, 1982. It was eerie because it was as if the hospital just walked away, leaving behind its gurneys, iron beds, barber chair, medical supplies in the cabinets, x-rays scattered on the floors, and

PHOTO COURTESY OF IAN MATHISEN

A photo of Essex Mountain Sanatorium as it is today. In the early twentieth century, it was a state-of-the-art facility helping thousands of tuberculosis patients.

specimens in labeled jars: a brain, a heart, a slice of lung, even a tapeworm removed from a forty-year-old woman. It seemed as if the sanatorium was evacuated overnight, instead of over time.

The famed treatment institution slowly rotted away and was vandalized for decades by both curiosity seekers and degenerates. Bodies were found there, and hate groups had meetings there. People would lock kittens in crawl spaces and starve them to death there, Essex County SWAT teams would put up paper targets and practice with paintballs there, and then there was an illegal dumping scandal that shook up the county and led to several officials being charged and jailed.

Ghost stories from trespassers who risked jail time and a $150 ticket told of their encounters, like vacant wheelchairs moving indoors on their own without any breeze around, hearing footsteps running down stairs with no earthy figure to explain it, faces in vacant windows, glowing blue lights just hovering in midair then darting off at eighty miles per hour. All these and hundreds more stories made their way into local folklore and Web sites. The chapel of many unanswered prayers just sat there vacant with no soul.

So just like Overbrook, its downhill neighboring asylum, the abandoned sanatorium was used as a way to make money through media fame. The place was rented out for the Sylvester Stallone movie *Cop Land*. Scenes of Michael Rapaport running through the woods with Harvey Keitel and crew chasing him, and a few scenes with Stallone walking around the grounds were now a part of this legendary facility's history. And not to be out-done, some scenes from the HBO series *The Sopranos* were shot there as well before the buildings were torn down.

While many politicians felt tearing down the buildings was the right thing to do to utilize the land and bring in revenue to the county, historians felt it was a shame that many of these historic buildings were not saved as landmarks. In 1993 the sana-torium was eligible to be included on the National Register of Historic Places, but the county did not follow up on it.

Now cleared of all structures, the plot is developing into a prime recreation and nature study reservation. The land hous-ing the sanatorium, asylum, and the many abandoned buildings associated with them had become Essex County's most legendary location while the facilities were active, and it remained so after they were abandoned.

But the other legend that cannot be missed, the hidden legend, is that of our two sweet determined women, the unsung heroes, two little housewives who shook up the county at a time in history when it was an unheard of thing to do—and they won. It's because of their dedication and relentlessness that they brought five hundred men to their way of thinking and in the end wound up creating a refuge for thousands of sick people and making the name of Essex County known around the world. This is the true legend of Essex County Mountain Sanatorium.

CHAPTER 8

The Walking Dead of Gully Road

Newark residents did not dare to walk down Gully Road after dark, even if accompanied by a priest with a Bible spraying holy water on their heads. It was considered haunted, and people would rather go a mile out of their way than risk deadly encounters on that road. Gully Road was known to be haunted by not one, but four ghosts, all who had no trouble making their presence known.

When you normally think of ghost stories and haunted sites, you think of dark, desolate streets, barren woods, or dark alleys, not a street right in the middle of one of the most populated areas in New Jersey. Such is the case of the famed street known as Gully Road.

Gully Road, known as one of the most haunted roads in American history, was located in Woodside, an area between Newark and Belleville along the Passaic River. It was located in the southern portion of Woodside, a beautiful village with well-manicured lawns and tree-lined streets. The road itself was a natural path that led down to the Passaic River and joined up with Washington Avenue, which is now Broadway, intersected with River Road, and went north along the town of Belleville. The road, which was used by the Lenni-Lenape Indians, was a path to the river. It was a dark, old, sunken road and it appears on the town's earliest maps.

Although all of River Road and some of Gully Road have been destroyed over time, and urbanization has led Route 21 and the Erie-Lackawanna Railroad tracks to cover the historic path, a small portion of it still remains in what is known as Herbert Place. But the street fragments are not what make Gully Road famous—it's the former inhabitants who were not happy to leave their homes and thus refused to leave.

The first set of phantoms is an unhappy old couple. They were some of the early settlers on Gully Road. They built their home, a quaint cottage at the cross streets of Gully Road and Washington Avenue. As the town grew the village decided it needed to widen the road so the new wider wagons could have access to the river. The only problem was that the old couple had their cottage right in the middle of where they needed to build. The townspeople ordered the couple to vacate their home . . . but they refused to leave the home they loved. This angered the townspeople and put a lot of stress on the couple. The townspeople made it very uncomfortable for the couple; the wife couldn't take the stress, had a heart attack, and died. This made the old man very bitter and more determined than ever to stay. The townspeople decided to force him out and started to tear the house down with him in it! He had to flee his home when the roof caved in on him. Shortly thereafter, he passed away. But he and his wife decided if they couldn't get what they wanted in this life, maybe in the afterlife they could . . . so they chose to hang around the street forever, perennially searching for their demolished cottage.

There have long been posthumous sightings of the couple, but the old man seems to be more active. Reports have been made of a bent-over old man suddenly darting into the street late at night, causing an unsuspecting motorist to swerve or jam on the brakes to avoid hitting him. For those with slower reflexes who have "hit" the old man, he vanishes as the car drives through him, leaving the driver shaken, with a ghost story to tell.

Supposedly the old man is trying to slow down traffic near his old abode, maybe in hopes that the story will end differently and the house will not be torn down. On one occasion, however, the old man actually became a messenger. An old couple had just had a fight. The ill husband begged his wife not to go out. But she got in the car and started to drive. The old ghost darted out in front of the lady's car and held up his hand for her to stop. She drove right through him. She was so shaken up, she returned home, just in time to be with her husband who was passing over to the other side. Coincidence, or one ghost doing a favor for another soon-to-be spirit?

Soon after, sightings of a second Gully Road ghost were reported. This time it was of a British spy, a Tory during the

Revolutionary War (1775–1783). He was captured by a group of Americans as he was caught spying on the shipping fleets along the river. Tried on the spot, he was hung from a tree at the bend of the road on Gully Hill. Apparently the hanging didn't dampen his personality, because he is the only happy ghost on the block, often caught playing harmless pranks on unsuspecting visitors who cross his path.

The third ghost was equally as disturbing in real life as she was in the afterlife. Mary Rowe, more commonly known as Moll DeGrow, was not a pleasant woman. Alive during the mid-1800s, she was known in town as a witch. No one knows who started the rumor, but she was blamed for everything bad that occurred. If milk went sour or a puppy died, it was Moll's fault. Horses were known to bolt away after midnight never to return again if they saw her. Dogs would bark viciously. Parents would use the rumor that a witch lived on the block as a way to keep their kids in at night. Over the years her reputation grew. Her acts became more evil and there was talk that she was practicing devil worship. Soon however, things took a really bad turn: Healthy babies who had set eyes upon her suddenly started to die without cause, though people said this curse only affected families Moll had some sort of grudge against.

The townspeople got fed up and decided to lead a mob, Frankenstein style, to her broken down shack. With torches burning they were ready to dispose of the witch. But Moll beat them to the punch. When they broke down the door, there she was, sitting in a chair, dead, with a wide evil grin on her face. Upset they didn't carry out the deed themselves, they were glad to be rid of her nonetheless, or so they thought. They buried her in Mount Pleasant Cemetery (a new burial site at the time). Legend has it that anyone who lights an open flame (torches, candles, campfires) near the burial site will see it inexplicably go out.

And last but not least, what ghost street would be complete without a devil sighting? This, however, is not a Jersey Devil sighting, but the true villain himself, the archangel.

As the story goes, in the 1860s a young boy wanted more than anything else to be a sailor. His parents were not happy about this, but agreed to let him go on a trial run on a local schooner that was captained by a local Belleville resident. If he liked it, they would let the boy become a sailor. If he wasn't good at it, he'd go into his father's business.

The boy took to the life of a sailor right away, and the old salt agreed to take him on as crew. One night as they were heading back home, a huge storm struck and the captain was forced to dock the boat in Newark. Being a rough old man, he decided to walk home with the boy to Belleville through thunder and lightning. The captain, who could not utter a sentence without cursing, was belting out a string of profanities. This made the boy extremely uncomfortable, because his parents were very strict. As they were walking he noticed the captain had decided to take a shortcut, right through the dreaded Gully Road. The boy questioned the captain about going down the road. "Boy, you're not scared of some ghost stories, are you?" the captain said. The boy did not want to reveal his fear, so he followed the captain, constantly looking over his shoulders for any one of the ghostly residents.

As he kept walking, he had the strange sensation he was being watched. He kept turning around to see if anyone else was crazy enough to be on these streets in the height of a torrential downpour. As the lightning flashed he saw a priest in full garb and figured he had nothing to fear. When the next strike of lightning hit, he saw the priest again, but he noticed two strange things. One, the man was not wet at all, and two, every time the captain swore up a verbal storm the priest would laugh out loud, so loud that the boy was amazed the captain didn't hear.

He kept trying to get the captain's attention, to make him stop . . . but each time he did, the captain swore louder and just kept on walking. Finally the boy was able to get the captain's attention and force him to stop and look at the strange man following them.

The captain saw the man and started to go over to him. Just then another lightning bolt lit up the sky. It was then that both of them noticed that the clergyman's legs ended in hooves, that two small horns protruded from his head, and that despite his laugh, his eyes were red with the fires of hell. They both ran until they were off Gully Road and onto River Road, with the devil far behind. They got to the captain's house and had a drink to calm their nerves.

The next day the captain told the boy's parents that their son would make a fine sailor.

They went back to the ship, taking the long route and bypassing Gully Road. They felt no need to share the street with demons from beyond.

The legends of Gully Road still live on. Since the turn of the twentieth century the roads have been filled in, the streets paved, and streetlights added. Manicured lawns have been replaced by an automotive store and a Christian ministry, but the road still has a creepy feel to it. The road at the end is blocked off so cars cannot travel down it anymore, although if you go on

PHOTO COURTESY OF FRAN CAPO

Said to be the most haunted street in New Jersey, today Gully Road is called Herbert Place. Off to the right is the gate to Mount Prospect Cemetery, where the witch Moll DeGrow is buried.

the sidewalk you can walk through an old open gate that leads into Mount Pleasant Cemetery.

Although most current residents have no knowledge of the street's history, one local resident, Edwin, who has lived there for five years, says that when he walks his dog at night he hears footsteps coming toward him from the cemetery, but sees no one. His dog barks and tries to go after the footsteps. He also mentioned that a friend of his spotted a young boy and girl on the street at night outside the gate dressed in Dutch clothes.

The street that is now known as Herbert Place was named after the famous fiction writer, Henry William Herbert, who lived there. His pen name was Frank N. Forrester, and apparently he had the same type of personality as old Moll DeGrow. It seems only fitting that he is buried at the same graveyard.

Recent visitors to the cemetery have reported ghosts playing tricks on them, and photographers have also noted ghostly orbs that always appear in one particular part of the graveyard, balls of light representing the dear departed.

One thing is for sure, the ghosts are still lurking around, and aren't shy about letting people know it. Apparently they want the legend to continue, and so it does. Until then . . . when you drive down a charming wooded street that reminds you of Andy Griffith's Mayberry, just remember—evil may lurk around the next corner.

CHAPTER 9

The Boogeyman of Westfield

For a month, Shirley Cunnick had been observing the nineteen-room, three-story Victorian mansion known as Breeze Knoll. It was one of the classiest homes in Westfield, located at 431 Hillside Avenue. People would often drive by just to admire it. But something did not feel right. She watched as the lights in the home slowly burned out one by one, and she would hear a faint eerie music playing all day long. Occasionally she would see a strange car drive by very slowly. Sometimes the car would park and just sit in front of the house. She knew the family was on vacation and that it wasn't their car, but it was more than that. The feeling of uneasiness kept eating away at her. Soon she would find out her instincts were right.

The home belonged to forty-six-year-old John Emil List, a quiet, meticulous accountant who kept to himself and barely ever smiled. He liked being in control and was the type to mow his lawn in a suit and tie. Any fears, frustrations, or anger he had he repressed inward and let the world and his family think everything was fine. As a devout churchgoing Lutheran, he believed in God, and wanted to only do what was right in the eyes of the Lord. For months he had been praying for an answer. He had failed time and time again and was fired from various jobs, not because he did not do them well, but because he just didn't quite fit in. As a result he was way behind on his mortgage payments, was making less than $5,000 for the entire year, and was facing bankruptcy and foreclosure. His forty-five-year-old wife, Helen, was sick with syphilis, a disease she got from her first husband, was no longer going to church, and was an alcoholic. She had developed cerebral atrophy (her brain was shrinking) and John was told to have her institutionalized, but being a devoted husband he refused. He wanted to keep the family together. In addition he felt his three teenage kids, sixteen-year-old Patty, fifteen-year-old John Jr., and thirteen-year-old Frederick were not responding well to his rigid ways. His elderly mother, Alma, lived in the attic; she had sold her house in Bay City, Michigan, and then lent him the money for the gorgeous home they were living in. She was loving but overbearing. List calculated all his options. Finally he found his answer. It was simple. He knew he could do it. In fact, he felt he had to do it. He had to murder his family. The reason he came up with was simple: He had to save their souls.

He developed a meticulous plan. In October 1971, he applied for firearms registration for "home protection." He had a 1912 Steyr automatic 9 mm handgun that had belonged to his late father and a .22-caliber pistol left over as a souvenir from his war days. He wanted to make sure the guns were legal. To distract himself from his family woes and financial stresses, he turned to hobbies, like reading books on military strategy, crime, and weapons. He casually mentioned to his brother-in-law that it would be easy for someone like him, an accountant with access to numerous Social Security numbers, to pick up and start a new life.

On November 5, 1971, after enjoying a family meal, List gathered his three children for a family chat. He told them that they must prepare to die. He wanted to know how they wanted their bodies to be handled, asking them point blank if they would rather be buried or cremated. They told their father they would rather be buried. He nodded and walked out of the kitchen.

Patty, the oldest daughter and the most "rebellious" one, decided to confide in her community workshop drama teacher, Mr. Ed Illiano. She told him, "If you ever hear that my dad says we are going on a long vacation, that means he is planning on killing us." The teacher found it an odd thing to hear. He wasn't sure if this was Patty's overactive imagination, or just drama from a drama student having some family disputes. He quickly dismissed her comment.

List originally thought the best chance for his family's souls to go to heaven was to kill them on All Saints Day, but his mother-in-law got sick and delayed the murder plans. But that gave him a new semi-true cover story.

His new date was now set: November 9, 1971. He made sure all home deliveries of newspapers, mail, and milk would be stopped, saying that the family would be going away on vacation. He mailed himself a "special delivery" letter that contained a key to one of his filing cabinet drawers, the drawer where he planned to keep the murder weapons after the deed was done.

That cold November morning he went to the garage and loaded his guns. Despite the request to halt deliveries, the milkman came by unexpectedly, but he read a note List had posted on the door just in case and did not leave the milk. It was now 9:00 a.m. List felt the coast was clear. He went into the kitchen where his wife Helen was dressed in a red satin robe. She was staring out the window eating her morning toast. List walked up behind her and held the 9 mm gun eighteen inches from the back of her head. As she turned to look at him, he shot her on the left side of the face. She died instantly, with toast jammed in the back of her throat. He fired two more bullets into the wall. Blood oozed out onto the linoleum floor. He left her there for the moment. His mission had begun.

Next he went up the back staircase to make his way to his mother's third-floor apartment. He walked in without knocking. His mother was startled and turned to him with a plate in her hand. She asked what the commotion was downstairs. He smiled and kissed her. Then he shot her in the left eye. Again he shot two more bullets into the wall. His mother dropped into a kneeling position and then fell backwards on the floor, causing her kneecaps to break underneath her weight. The impact of her body hitting the floor caused her false teeth to pop out and break.

His plan was to drag her downstairs and place her with his wife, but when he started to move her, he realized she was too heavy for him. He looked around and decided instead to roll her into a carpet runner and shove her body into a storage area. Compulsively concerned with being neat, List tried to clean the blood with a towel, but traces were left.

List then went back down to the kitchen and dragged Helen forty feet by the legs into the ballroom. He decided the floor was too cold for her, so he took out three sleeping bags and opened them up side by side. He placed Helen face down on the sleeping bag. Then he covered her with a bath towel and placed another towel over the back of her head.

He tried to clean up the trail of blood, but it was grueling work. He realized he was stained in blood and had to be presentable when the kids came home so they would not suspect anything. So he went into his wife's bedroom (he had a separate room) and wiped the blood on her sheets. Although he did not regret what he was doing, it did make him a bit queasy, so he vomited in the toilet. In doing so, he left a bloody handprint on the lid.

Then he gathered himself, showered, and changed into a fresh business suit. Refreshed, he had some time before the kids came home to continue his well-thought-out plan.

Next on the agenda was a note to his boss at State Mutual Life Assurance, saying he had to go on an unexpected trip to North Carolina with his family to visit his mother-in-law, who was ill. Her illness was actually a blessing in disguise for her because she was supposed to visit, but couldn't and was saved from becoming another "soul saved" by List.

List then wrote the same excuse note to the children's teachers, afterschool programs, and to Patty's and Fred's afterschool employers. This excuse would give him some time to escape after the deed was done. With the notes written, he still had some time on his hands before the kids came home, so he did what any "good" man would do—he mowed the lawn in his suit and tie.

A slight change in plans came when Patty called from her job at Duke's Subs and Deli on South Avenue. She said she needed a ride home. He picked her up, and then made sure he got into the house before she did. He quickly hid behind the door, and then shot her in the back of the head with the .22-caliber gun. She too died instantly. He then dragged her to the ballroom and laid her on the sleeping bag next to her mom.

There were only two children now left to kill. He still had some time before the next two were due home. So he cleaned himself of blood once again and continued with his list of things to do. He went to the post office to mail the letters, withdrew $2,000 from his mother's and his joint bank account, ate a sandwich, and then waited for the kids.

He picked up Fred from his afterschool job, and repeated the same routine he had used with Patty: ran into the house first, hid behind the door, shot him in the back of the head, dragged him to the ballroom, laid him on a sleeping bag, and cleaned up the blood. Both also had their heads covered with a towel.

Now all he had left was John Jr. John was at a soccer game. Here's where there are two differing accounts of what happened. According to the TV crime network Tru TV and excerpts from the book *Righteous Carnage* by Timothy Benford, John Jr. came home early from the soccer game, entered from the laundry room, and surprised the senior List. However, in an interview with List himself on *American Justice,* John recalls, "I decided to pick John up at school so I could watch the soccer game. He seemed to be enjoying it. We came home together in the car." Then John Jr. placed his gym bag on the kitchen counter and unzipped his coat. He happened to turn and see his father coming at him with the gun. List shot at his son, but he did not drop like the others. They both struggled with the gun. A bullet fired into the ceiling, two shots went into the floor, one hit the cabinet, and another hit the dining room window frame.

John Jr. tried to run, but List shot him in the back, neck, and head. Weakened from the gunshot wounds, the boy fell to the floor and broke his jaw, yet he was still alive. He tried to crawl across the floor to escape, and his father, now desperate to kill him, started firing at him with both guns. He fired one shot right into his eye . . . yet he was still not dead. Finally, after he was pumped with ten bullets, he died. List later said he felt "relaxed that his mission was finally complete." The last of his family members was dragged to the ballroom. He covered John Jr.'s face with a towel. The children lay side by side on the sleeping bags; Helen was placed perpendicular at the top of their heads, making a letter T.

Then List did what any God-fearing man would do. He knelt down and prayed for each one of them. Then he bid their souls farewell and said he wished they would depart in peace. He was now certain they would all go to heaven together as a family. When asked later why he didn't kill himself and take the journey with his family, he said, "Suicide is a mortal sin, not forgiven by God. I didn't want to go to hell." He was certain that when he died he would be forgiven by God and his family and he would be reunited with them in heaven. With his mind at ease, he then tidied up the place.

At seven that night, he called his pastor, Reverend Rehwinkel, at Redeemer Evangelical Lutheran Church, and told him that he was headed to North Carolina with his family and that he would not be able to teach his Sunday school class. The reverend understood and said he would keep his family in his prayers. List then called Patty's drama teacher and told him they suddenly had to go out of town. The call ran a chill up the teacher's spine. Patty's words echoed in his head.

List now sat down at his desk and composed a five-page letter on yellow legal pad paper to the one person he trusted most in the world, the pastor he had called earlier. He felt he owed him a complete explanation.

In the confessional letter, dated November 9, 1971, he took full responsibility for the murders. He stated his frustrations, wrote the reason for the killings was to "spare them the sinful effects of poverty," expressed condolences to family members, gave advice to associates, and outlined the burial arrangements he wanted for his family. It was a thorough confession. He told the reverend that he knew God would forgive him. He ended the letter with an eerie postscript. "P.S. Mother is in the hallway in the attic—3rd floor. She was too heavy to move." Then he simply signed it "John."

He left several other letters taped to the filing cabinets, including one addressed to the pastor telling of the location of keys, one to his mother-in-law, and one to his boss.

After the day's gruesome events, he sat down in the kitchen and had another meal. Then he cleaned up in the kitchen, fed the pet fish, and went to sleep in the billiard room in the basement.

That same night, while List slept, Patty's drama teacher, Ed Illiano, drove by Breeze Knoll just to make sure everything was okay. He saw some lights on and figured everything was fine. He dismissed the thought, at least for a while.

The next morning, before John fled to begin his new life, the mailman slipped the special delivery letter that contained the key he had mailed to himself under the door. List pretended he wasn't home. He had a few more details to attend to, to make sure he had taken care of his family properly. He turned down the thermostat to 50 degrees to keep the bodies from decomposing. He turned on lights in various rooms to make it look like people were home. He also turned on a recorder that played a loop tape of his favorite classical music, over and over again. The only way the music would turn off was if someone physically turned it off. He made sure it was loud enough to be heard in the street to deter intruders from coming in. Then he took his passport and one suitcase full of clothes and drove his Chevy Impala to John F. Kennedy Airport in Queens. He left it in long-term parking. The car at the airport was a diversionary tactic. He left it there to make anyone looking for him think that he left by plane. Instead, he boarded a train to Denver where he already had rented a trailer to enjoy the Rocky Mountains for a while. He knew the car at the airport would buy him time, but he had no idea how much time. It ultimately took eighteen years to find him.

He changed his name to Robert P. Clark and got a job as a nighttime cook at a Holiday Inn in the outskirts of Denver. He knew they would come after him soon enough, but he felt it was the job of the police to find him, and not his job to turn himself in. As he put it, "I was thankful to be living a free life. I didn't want to be incarcerated if it wasn't necessary."

Meanwhile, the drama coach was getting concerned. Patty had a rehearsal for an upcoming play and had not bothered to contact the coach to tell him when she was planning on coming back. This was unlike her. He asked a friend on the police force to investigate, but without any evidence of wrongdoing, they couldn't secure a search warrant and nothing happened. But Illiano was determined to find out what was going on.

Finally, on December 7, 1971, a full month after the murders were committed, Illiano decided to act. This time he wasn't going to just drive by slowly; he was going to knock on the door. He drove his car, the same car that the neighbor, Shirley Cunnick, kept seeing on occasion, to the house. He brought a friend with him, Barbara Sheridan, for backup. They rang the doorbell and waited. No answer. So they went back to his car that was parked in the driveway to decide what to do next. Meanwhile, Cunnick couldn't take it anymore. Her gut feelings had been bothering her for weeks now, and seeing this car yet again was the last straw. She called the police to report the car, and sent her husband out to detain Illiano and Sheridan by talking to them.

Entering the List house, the police sensed something was wrong. They heard the funereal, looped music over the intercom. The place was cold and barren, with a terrible smell. As they walked through the house they noticed what appeared to be blood stains on the walls. They followed the blood-stained trail to the ballroom. The decomposing bodies lay there for all to see. The mother's nightgown was high above her thighs and they could see her stomach was badly distended. Illiano immediately identified the bodies, and police backup was called. The officers continued to search the house. Forty-five minutes later they found the grandmother's body upstairs. An expression of horror was frozen on her face. Bloody newspapers and towels were found in the kitchen and ballroom.

They noticed that the only body missing was that of John List. He immediately became a suspect. Within an hour, a Tele-type alarm was sent out for him. Meanwhile, Chief James Moran had the bodies sent for an autopsy and evidence was gathered. List's car was found in the JFK parking lot with a voucher dated November 10th, but no record of him taking any flights was found. The FBI took over the case from there. The case became the second most infamous crime in New Jersey history, next to that of the Lindbergh Baby. A nationwide manhunt was launched, hundreds of leads checked, but all without results.

The family was buried in Fairview Cemetery in cheap metal caskets, while List's mother was buried in Michigan. Dozens of police were on hand at both the funerals and the burial site to see if List would show up, but he didn't.

Wanted fliers were sent out with List's picture and physical description. Pharmacies were contacted since List suffered from hemorrhoids and the FBI thought they could catch him if he filled a prescription. Eye doctors were contacted since he wore glasses. Nothing turned up.

Since the List murder was all over the news, everyone knew the massacre had occurred in the now-abandoned mansion, and it became a place for morbid curiosity seekers. On August 30,

1972, nine months after the murders, the place was burned to the ground. The police originally thought it was some drunken careless teenagers who had been holding séances in the ballroom, but it turned out to be the work of an arsonist who was never found. Destroyed along with the home was the ballroom's stained glass skylight, rumored to be a signed Tiffany original worth over $100,000. Had List only looked up when he was thinking about his options, he could have sold the skylight and might have been out of debt, instead of out of family. After all, his home only cost $50,000 at the time of purchase.

Meanwhile, Robert "Bob" Clark, formerly known as John List, was getting bolder, feeling that maybe he wouldn't be caught after all. By 1975 he had joined the St. Paul's Lutheran Church in Denver, gotten a driver's license, and bought a car. In 1985 he married a woman named Delores Miller and told her that his previous wife had died of cancer. But patterns always repeat. He started getting fired from jobs and was asked to leave as a Sunday school teacher because he was too rigid and strict with the children. Wife number two was now complaining about Robert and wanted to leave him. Robert started to complain to a neighbor, Wanda Flannery.

Unfortunately for him, Wanda liked to read the tabloids. One day, while paging through one, she spotted a story about a man named John List who had murdered his family and gotten away with it. The more she read, the more she started to feel uneasy. Bob and John List seemed to have a lot in common; they looked similar, and both had the same mastoidectomy scar behind their right ears. They had trouble holding down jobs, were avid churchgoers, wore suits and ties, and were from Michigan. She started to get nervous, and decided she had to make Delores aware of the situation. She went over to their home and showed her the paper, saying, "Just show him the article and see how he reacts." Delores agreed, but instead threw the paper out. The neighbor was convinced Bob was John, but could do nothing. Shortly after, Bob packed up Delores and relocated to Richmond, Virginia.

Meanwhile the police, even though the case was cold, were determined not to let this ruthless killer get away. Detective Jeffrey Paul Hummel, who worked in the Major Crimes unit for the prosecutor's office in Union County, was assigned to the case in 1985. In May of that year, he decided to try a new method to catch List. He decided to go to a psychic, Elizabeth Lerner. While at the time the information she gave him was not of much help, in hindsight she was extremely accurate. The psychic said that List had not traveled by plane, but left by train or bus and that he fled somewhere southwest. She said the state of Virginia held some significance. She also said he remarried and the woman had something to do with Baltimore. (That's where List married Delores.) Shortly after the visit with the psychic, Hummel was moved to another case and Captain Frank Marranca took it over.

Hummel, meanwhile, always stayed interested in the case. In 1988 he saw a new TV show called *America's Most Wanted* hosted by John Walsh. The show asked the public for help in tracking criminals. Hummel suggested to Marranca that they try to get the List case on the show.

They approached the show, but were told the case was too old. But Marranca would not give up. He was determined to make John List pay for his horrific crime. He found out that the show's producer, Michael Linder, was doing a talk near him, so he re-presented the file. Linder was convinced and during episode #66, an eight-minute segment on John List was set to air.

Now all they needed was a recent photo. But the only one they had was of List at the age of nineteen. So they did something rarely done on the show. Linder hired a sculptor, Frank Bender, to do an aged clay bust of him on the show. Bender worked side by side with Richard Walter, a criminal psychologist who studied personality traits. Together they decided what List would look like and created the bust for the show. The final touch was a pair of glasses. New Jersey's most famous murder case, and the oldest cold case ever aired on the show, was seen by twenty-two million viewers on May 12, 1989.

Oddly enough, *America's Most Wanted* was one of List's favorite shows. He often encouraged others to watch it, and he always wondered if some day his mug would appear on the show. On that particular day he missed half of the show because he and Delores had gone to church. He came in at the tail end of the program and recognized himself. He was "surprised the bust of him was so accurate. He didn't realize they had that technology." He hoped none of his neighbors were watching, but they were.

Three hundred phone calls came pouring in. Lieutenant Bernard Tracy from Westfield, who had been on the case, missed the crucial call. That call was instead rerouted to the FBI in Richmond, Virginia. Watching the show that night was the tabloid-loving neighbor from Denver, Wanda Flannery. Even though she felt the bust didn't look exactly like Bob, she had her son-in-law call the show and give them Bob's new address in Virginia. She believed in her heart that Bob Clark and John List were one and the same person.

On June 1, 1989, eleven days later, the FBI showed up at the Richmond home with a flyer. List's stunned wife answered the door. She told them that there was no way they were the same person, and she was so confident she gave them List's address at work. They immediately went to his office. He did not act surprised to see them. He did not resist, but he denied that he was John List. He was arrested, taken to the police station, and fingerprinted. The prints matched. List still denied it was him even with all the evidence staring him in the face.

On June 29, 1989, he was extradited from Virginia to New Jersey. The bail was set at $1 million. When he got off the plane it was a media circus. The people of New Jersey had waited a long time for this day and the world was watching.

Since they had the confessional letter, 150 pieces of evidence from the crime scene, and the matching fingerprints, there was no question they had their man. It was now just a question of whether it was premeditated or the act of a lunatic. The prosecution wanted a first-degree murder charge, but the defense wanted a second-degree murder charge, with the reason of insanity attached to the plea.

On March 26, 1990, at 7:29 p.m., psychiatrist and witness for the prosecution Steven Simring began a four-hour mental evaluation of List. Simring said: "List was mild mannered, courteous, soft spoken. He was very precise and exact. He had no remorse or superficial

This composite sketch was used by police in their hunt for John List. Lieutenant Bernard Tracy handed out hundreds of copies.

PHOTO COURTESY OF THE WESTFIELD POLICE RECORDS DEPARTMENT

regret." List simply told Simring, "Something had to happen that was unfortunate." Simring concluded, "He (List) had OCD but no major mental illness, no psychiatric disorder, no psychological excuse whether to excuse or to mitigate, he was not on autopilot. He always had a choice and was mentally capable of executing that choice." Simring continued, "Mr. List had been suffering from a 'midlife' crisis when he slaughtered his family and he enjoyed life in the years afterward." In other words, Simring was convinced the defense could not use mental incompetence as their argument to get the sentence reduced. The defense tried to play up the fact that List was the result of an authoritarian father who taught him to care for and protect his family at all costs, which meant he could never allow them to go on welfare.

The trial began on April 5, 1990. List was sixty-four years old at the time. Eleanor Clark, the prosecutor for the state, told the courtroom of List's meticulous plans. The defense attorney, Elijah Miller, pressed for a change of venue, but he had to do this in the name of John List, not Robert Peter Clark, and the request was denied. Miller argued that List had to have been mentally ill in order to commit the murders and that he couldn't have deviated from his course of action if he had wanted to. The defense also tried to keep the confession letter out of evidence. But it was admitted in.

A psychiatrist for the defense, Dr. Sheldon Miller, testified that because List "grew up without developing the skills needed to deal with problems as they arose, he knew only two places to look, to his father's directives and to his understanding of his Lutheran faith. He was stuck in a closed circuit. He was like an elastic band that is stretched until it cannot stretch any more and finally snaps."

Seven short days later, on April 12, 1990, List's fate was decided. The jury took just nine hours to deliver their verdict. List was convicted of murder in the first degree. On May 1, 1990, at the Union County Courthouse in Elizabeth, New Jersey, Judge

William L. E. Wertheimer sentenced him to five consecutive life terms in prison. Then something happened in the courtroom that had never happened before. Applause broke out. It took eighteen years, five months, and twenty-two days to capture the monster, but they finally did and people were relieved.

List showed no remorse and said he felt no guilt. After sentencing, however, List did read a public statement of remorse: "I'm truly sorry for the tragedy that happened in 1971. I feel that due to my mental state at the time I was unaccountable for what happened."

List tried for an appeal on the grounds that his judgment at the time of the murder was impaired due to post-traumatic stress disorder from being a veteran of World War II and the Korean War. He also argued that the letter to his pastor should have been kept private.

Meanwhile, he seemed to be relatively happy in jail. He said that he felt safer in prison, rather than on the outside "where people kill people at random." Add to that the fact that in prison he had no bills to worry about, and his life was regimented and orderly, just the way he liked it. When asked, List said "he wasn't worried that he never would get parole, because he feels he had his parole before he got arrested." Until his dying day he stated that "he would go to heaven and that his family would forgive him for whatever harm they did to each other on earth."

List served eighteen years in the New Jersey State Prison in Trenton. He died at the age of eighty-two in St. Francis Medical

Center in Trenton four days after he was sent there from prison. He had a massive blood clot obstructing the blood flow to his lungs. The coroner listed the cause of death as "pneumonia." The date of his death was March 21, 2008; ironically, it was Good Friday. When the Newark *Star-Ledger* reported his death they referred to him as the "Boogeyman of Westfield." The name stuck.

No one came to claim his body. None of his relatives or his wife Dolores wanted it. But ultimately he was buried next to his mother, the very mother that he had murdered, in Frankenmuth, Michigan.

Meanwhile, back in Westfield, even though a new house now stands at the scene of the murders, neighbors still refer to it as the "List House," and although there is no marker in front, the eerie story of the man and his murders remains a part of the town's history. The boogeyman is dead, but the legend lives on.

CHAPTER 10

The Robin Hood of the Pine Barrens

When you think of Robin Hood, you think of an attractive man in green tights, a hat with a feather, and booties, who carries a bow, arrows, and a sword, and lives in Sherwood Forest with his merry men. Oh yes, and he'd be good with the ladies.

Supposedly, a real-life Robin Hood existed in the Pine Barrens of New Jersey, and his name was Joe Mulliner. Over the years, the stories about this man kept getting wilder and wilder, but one thing is true: He did exist. But no one is quite sure just how much of a Robin Hood he was, as the line between fact and fiction has blurred over the years.

Not much is actually known of Mulliner in the early years. In fact, the exact day and even year he was born has been lost in the history books. His time of birth has been estimated to be sometime in the 1740s, although one of his grave sites reads BORN 1750. (There are in fact two grave sites, and no one is sure which is the true site.) However, it is known that Joe was a Tory outlaw, and his legendary exploits occurred during the time of the Revolutionary War.

He came from a good family, had two brothers, and was born somewhere in South Jersey. He was well educated, handsome, friendly, good humored, and was huge with brute strength to match. Reports have him at six feet five inches tall. He had a deep booming laugh that would echo wherever he went. With all these attributes it's easy to see how this guy was the life of the party.

At one of the parties, Mulliner met his wife, whose name has been difficult to confirm. He asked her to marry him and they settled down on a small farm that had a beautiful view of the Mullica River. (Today that area is known as Pleasant Mills.)

The two were very happy. He was a coastal pilot and made a decent living. Then the war broke out. As a result, his reputation as a good, decent man was about to change. He went from pilot to pirate.

His brothers went off and joined the American side of the Revolution, the colonial army. Mulliner, however, was a loyalist. He, like many other New Jersey residents, remained loyal to the King of England. This was a problem because his neighbors were for independence. As the war raged on, living next to neighbors with different political views was not so easy, especially when he made his position as a Tory well known. In fact, at one point they nicknamed him the "Englishman," not for his birthright but for his political loyalty.

In 1779, to avoid arrest, he was forced to flee the farm. His wife stayed behind and miraculously was never bothered, which was highly unusual because the law of the day was to seize property of known Tories. Rumor has it that the farm belonged to Mulliner's wife's family and so the colonial government did not seize the property.

Mulliner now had to go into hiding. Where better to hide than in his own version of Sherwood Forest, a unique place called "The Forks," an island that sat in the middle of where the Mullica and Batsto Rivers merged. Conveniently it was only about a half mile from the farm that his wife was tending. It was a navigable waterway, yet inland and remote, a perfect hideout. It was surrounded by eerie swamps with a dense layer of tangled cedar woods that hid him from the authorities.

However, Joe wasn't the only one on this island. There were anywhere between thirty to one hundred men at any given time hiding there as well, including men in similar circumstances as Mulliner, and some common criminals. Towering over the others on the island and having a personality that could win friends and influence people, Mulliner quickly became the leader of the gang, and they called themselves aptly enough "The Refugees," which was also a common term for those fighting on the Loyalist side. Now he had his bandits who could also moonlight as pirates.

For his first part of his refugee career he took to the seas. He built a canoelike device by nailing some small cedar logs to a large log and used it to paddle to and from pre-set rendezvous points. With stealthlike precision, he'd go in and out of the coves along the Jersey Shore around Egg Harbor. From his lair he preyed upon vulnerable merchant ships as they dropped anchor. Sometimes he took crew members as hostages and then would collect a ransom from their relatives on land for their safe return. If he thought he might be caught, he would steer to a nearby woody area and he was instantly camouflaged. But he and his men soon got bored with capturing ships and went from sea to land.

During that time period, his band of men were robbing wagons, plundering farms, stealing from taverns, and in some cases burning houses. He wore a British officer's red uniform, and carried pistols wherever he rode. Joe was a neighborhood robber; he hit the towns of Old Tuckerton and looted along the stage roads in Pine Towns, Quaker Bridge, Washington, Green Bank, and Mount as well as any village big enough to have a hotel and a group of homes.

As a Tory he was supposedly loyal to the King, meaning his "enemies" were the revolutionaries who had no power in New Jersey, and certainly not in the Pine Barrens where he did most of his looting. Therefore, his gang took full advantage of the woody surroundings and often would surprise enemy stagecoaches and relieve them of their goods.

As time went by, his gang did not discriminate and they took from both British sympathizers as well as patriots. This didn't win him many friends, so the question of whether he was a "Robin Hood of the Pine Barrens" is still up for debate. Some stories tell of him burning houses and stealing from the rich and giving to the poor, but in most cases, the only people he shared with were his fellow bandits, not-so-merry men who were only loyal to themselves and their pilfering ways. Like a good pirate, he buried much of the gold and treasure that he took.

In 1780 his band of men robbed the home of an elderly rich widow by the last name of Bates without his knowledge. Mrs. Bates happened to come home as the men were heading out the door with her belongings. She started to scream and throw stones at the robbers. They couldn't keep her quiet so they tied her to a tree. She kept screaming, so they burned her house down. Mulliner got wind of this and was very disappointed in his men. After all, he had a reputation to uphold. A sum of $300 was mysteriously delivered to the widow's doorstep a short time later. Everyone, including her, believed it came from Mulliner himself as an apology. With that money she was able to rebuild the house. According to some accounts, he also returned all her possessions.

Another tale involving Mulliner as a Robin Hood figure took place at the tavern at Washington, one of his favorite jaunts. The tavern was located deep in the Wharton State Forest, beside a road from Quaker Bridge to Tuckerton where he often hijacked stagecoaches. As he was heading out for an afternoon drink, he saw a young woman crying outside the tavern in a wedding dress. He asked the fair maiden what was making her so sad. She pointed to a big burly man sitting by the window inside the tavern, and told Mulliner that she was being forced to marry him. When he looked to see who her husband-to-be was, he realized it was a past enemy who had been pursuing him for the bounty on his head. Joe nodded to the woman and told her not to worry. Then he disappeared.

When the wedding ceremony began Joe just watched. He was waiting for the perfect moment to make his entrance. As the girl was about to say "I do," a gunshot went off.

Everyone ducked. Joe looked the groom in the eyes, grinned, and simply said, "Leave or die!" The groom took off running. Joe then took the hand of the lovely maiden, and danced with her and all the other maidens in attendance all night long. Some say they heard Joe whisper to the bride-to-be of a place to rendezvous later, "one hundred yards out the back door of the tavern through the woods to the field, then on to the far side of the field behind the large pine." No one knows if they met there. The only evidence that all of this happened was a bullet hole that reports say could be seen in the roof a few feet south of the chandelier until the tavern came down. Unfortunately, all that remains of the tavern is a depression in the ground where the cellar used to be.

Not all men, however, were so willing to just leave their women's side. There was a story of a small, mild-mannered man who actually stood up to Joe. The setting this time was

Thompson's Tavern, which was about five miles northwest of the Washington Tavern in the town of Quaker Bridge on the Batsto River. It was a dark, rainy night and Joe once again got wind of a party in full swing. He entered the tavern and looked around, as he always did, to spot the prettiest woman in the place. Now as Joe normally did, he muscled his way in, pushing the male dance partner aside so he could dance with the lady. But this time instead of the man timidly moving out of the way, he slapped Joe in the face . . . a slap that was heard throughout the bar. The music stopped, and a hush fell over the tavern. Everyone was on edge getting ready to duck for the gunfight that was sure to follow. But instead, Joe with his great personality, let out a hearty laugh and bellowed, "So fearless a little bantam must have the best girl present." Then Joe shook the little man's hand, danced one dance with his partner, returned her without incident, danced with a few more girls, and then dashed off into the night. The next day the town was buzzing with the story of the gentleman bandit.

One of the most famous Mulliner stories goes that in the summer of 1781, he got so offended that he actually kidnapped a hostess who excluded him from her party just to teach her a lesson. Even if she had wanted to invite Joe there was no way to do it and face her party guests. Joe stole from the very people that were going to be at the party! They hated him and would capture him in an instant, so she chose to leave him off the list.

The party's hostess, the graceful and beautiful Honore Read, was the daughter of an ironmaster who resided in Batsto

Village. The party was being held in their home in Pleasant Mills. Mulliner was not intimidated by her considerable charm and personality, and he crashed the party, went in and abducted her, then rode off with her. He later returned her that night to her father. Only the two of them know what happened, because she never told. Joe's abduction of the hostess became the basis for Charles Peterson's 1855 bestselling novel *Kate Aylesford* about a spunky heroine known as "The Heiress of Sweetwater." Honore Read's white two-story house, complete with double chimneys and dormer windows, still stands today on the shores of Nescochague Lake. But instead of it having a marker with Honore Read's name on it, the sign in front says KATE AYLESFORD MANSION.

For Joe, women proved to be his Achilles' heel. That same summer, while looking for another party to crash, he got word of a dance happening at the Indian Cabin Mill Inn in New Columbia, later known as Nescochague and now as Nesco. Once again, it was a bold move to go to the dance, but nothing could stop him from his desire to laugh and do the two-step with the ladies.

As usual, he took two of his men and stationed them outside the tavern to act as lookouts. He went inside and up to the ballroom, was seen through the peephole, and was let in.

On this particular day, he danced with the wrong lady. The soldier who was accompanying the lady was not pleased with the outlaw and decided to do something about it. After Mulliner pushed him aside, he slipped out of the house and down the path to Columbia Road, where the local patriot militia was camped out. He told Captain Baylin where the famed Tory was located. Quietly they gathered outside and surrounded the place. When Joe came out they stormed him. For the first time in his life Joe was a prisoner. He was disarmed, captured, and taken in handcuffs to Woodbury, where he was charged with "banditry and high treason" for his professed loyalty to the King. As the New Jersey *Gazette* reported, he was convicted and sentenced to be "hung that very day." The trial was quick, since he had become the terror of that part of New Jersey with his robbing "all that fell in his way." "Both the Whigs and the Tories wanted him dead."

On August 8, 1781, Joe Mulliner of Egg Harbor was transported from his jail cell along with his coffin to the nearby Gallows Hill. (Today, Gallows Hill is a cemetery called Laurel Hill. It is located on Jacksonville Road in Burlington, West Jersey's capital.) The town watched as he was hung from a low limb of a buttonwood tree, near the scrub cedars along the Mullica River, commonly referred to as High Banks. His pirating days lasted from 1775 to 1781. There was no proof he ever killed anyone or even inflicted bodily harm. At the time of his hanging, he was not thought of as a folk hero, but as time went on his stories became legendary.

As for the rest of his refugee gang, it has been said that Captain Baylin pursued them in their home turf. He fought them in Hemlock Swamp, and after a long battle, brought them to bay. Others were hung as well, including an army deserter.

Now a private residence, this building in Nesco, New Jersey,
was once known as the Indian Cabin Mill Inn. Here, Joe Mulliner,
noted refugee and Robin Hood of the Pine Barrens, was captured in 1781.

According to the history books, Joe's body was sent home
and buried on his farm, with a tombstone that simply read JM. In
1850 supposedly some inebriated men dug up Joe's bones. The
ironmaster of the village, Jesse Richards, had the bones returned
and he gave them a proper burial with a tombstone that just read
JOE MULLINER. But the Indian King Fish and Hunt Club, headed
by Charles Dietz of Audubon, thought that Joe should have a
more fitting tombstone. So he put a new one up that simply read
THE GRAVE OF JOE MULLINER—HUNG 1781. Supposedly there are
two grave sites for Joe and people are not sure which is the real

one. One is supposed to be two miles up the road from the Kate Aylesford mansion in the backwoods. The tombstone is weathered and knocked down and now is an unmarked stone between two houses, just a few feet away from someone's driveway. There is a small path leading up to it that is covered with thorns along the way.

The other tombstone is located on Pleasant Mills–Weekstown Road, Route 43, two miles east of Pleasant Mills, on the south side of road. Joe apparently didn't want to stay inside either grave, for there have been many people who claim to have seen his ghost. Some suggest he is looking to reclaim his buried treasure. Others say they have seen the tall ghost with pistols drawn on the roads where he used to loot the stagecoaches. Still others say they can hear his laugh on a windless day in the Pine Barrens where he used to hang with his gang.

CHAPTER 11

The Dreaded Voyage of the Morro Castle

aptain Robert Wilmott was liked by many. He was an out-
going, respected old salt who enjoyed mingling with the
passengers and was considered a fair guy to work for. He was a
bit stern, but he knew his stuff, and people were confident with
his skills. Among passengers, this rotund fifty-six-year-old man
with cherublike cheeks was normally a jolly soul.

He had reason to be jolly. He was the captain of the *Morro
Castle,* a 508-foot, four-story steam turbo electric drive twin-
propeller beauty owned by the Ward line company, nicknamed
the "millionaire yacht." It had been built to the tune of $5
million in 1930, an enormous amount of money back then. It
could hold 489 passengers in first and second class and 240 crew
members. It was a luxury hotel at sea complete with gorgeous
dining, an abundance of edible delicacies, a promenade, writing
rooms, library, tea room, and ballroom.

The ship was built beginning in January 1929 and completed over one year later on August 15, 1930, with the help of

U.S. government money provided as an incentive to modernize maritime fleets to compete with foreign cruise liners. This passenger liner had its maiden voyage on August 23, 1930, with much fanfare, and completed its 1,100-mile trip in an impressive fifty-nine hours. It had been sailing happily from New York City to Havana, Cuba, ever since. It had made over one hundred successful trips with Captain Wilmott at the helm and he was very comfortable. With the company having over fifty years of service under its bow, it touted the tagline "The Ward line has lost but two ships, and it's never lost a passenger" as part of its advertising. Much as the *Titanic* had done, the Ward line bragged about their safety and speed, for the *Morro Castle* was supposed to be the finest of its day.

But the ticket price to board the *Morro Castle* was much lower than the *Titanic*'s, which ranged from $36.25 one way for a single person willing to share a cabin, to a first-class ticket starting at $125, to $4,500 per person for the deluxe suite. For $75 one could buy a round-trip ticket for five days on the *Morro Castle,* with a private cabin, which included all meals and a two-night stay in Havana. It was a trip that attracted both Cuban and American passengers. In fact, the price was so good that even during the Great Depression the ship remained relatively full. The ship became known as a party boat, or as they put it, a "whoopee cruise," for indeed the passengers could get something here that they couldn't get on American soil at the time: legal alcohol. The passengers of all classes took full advantage of the fact that once they got outside the three-mile Prohibition-enforced radius surrounding the United States, they could drink to their hearts' content at sea and in Cuba. On the return trip from Cuba, as the ship pulled away from the Morro Castle Fortress that had given the ship its name and guards the entrance to Havana Bay, the partying would continue. The festivities were especially big the night before they reached port in New York because all liquor had to be consumed before they crossed the three-mile line. So to accommodate the law, late-night partying was common for the vacationing passengers.

Once in port, however, with ticket prices so low, the turn-around time for the ship had to be quick in order to be profitable. They also carried cargo and mail in addition to passengers. Often the ship would come into New York on a Saturday morning, unload the cargo and passengers, and be ready to set sail that same evening. Captain Wilmott and senior officers got vacation time, but for the crew, it was a grueling job that paid only $30 a month. Many of them would sell bootleg liquor to compensate. There was also no time off to see their families, so many actually had to quit in order to have some home life and then hope that they would get rehired. Needless to say, there was a large turnover due to the schedule. The crew were not used to working together as one cohesive unit, and they didn't have any loyalty to one another or the officers. Each of them was just looking forward to the next payday. Because of these conditions, they were not the cream of the crop. To make matters worse, the

Ward Company had a reputation for firing their employees on the spot, and on the last trip alone fifty deckhands and stewards were replaced for various offenses.

But the captain was a happy man. He had been with the Ward Company for thirty-one years, and his reward was being the captain of this ship. People often joked with him, "What would you do if the ship was taken away from you?" He joked, "In that case, I'd take her with me." Apparently no truer words were ever said.

The cruise to Havana on September 1, 1934, started out almost like any other. Some crew members who knew the captain well noticed that he was not his usual jovial self. He seemed a bit preoccupied. Some passed it off as boredom, or maybe even stress. Rumors started to spread that there were arms on board being smuggled to Cuba. Some surmised that the captain might be worried that rebels in Cuba were thinking of the ship as a target.

By the time the ship was heading back to New York on September 6 for its three-day trek across the chilly Atlantic, the captain's demeanor seemed to have become chilly as well. His first concern was the weather: There was a nasty nor'easter storm brewing that would make the voyage back for the passengers uncomfortable. Second, his stomach had been bothering him lately; he had come down with food poisoning just a month earlier and he hadn't felt the same since. Third, before he left the port in Cuba, the Havana police chief told him that a Communist agent was believed to be aboard his ship, and that sabotage was likely to occur. Lastly, and worst of all, he felt that someone other than an agent was out to murder him and destroy the ship.

He confided in two people on the ship, Chief Officer William Warms (the second in command) and Chief Engineer Eban Abbott, that foul play was in the air. He told them he already had a suspect in mind, George Alanga, a hired assistant radio engineer from the Radio Marine Corporation (today known as RCA). Alanga had worked with Wilmott before and had tried to organize a strike for better conditions as the ship was about to set sail. His attempt was unsuccessful, but he had delayed the ship and caused disharmony on that previous cruise. Now Alanga was back aboard. In the captain's mind Alanga was dangerous, and thus the Ward Company had already notified Alanga that he would be dismissed when the ship returned to New York. Disgruntled and about to be fired, Alanga had nothing to lose if he caused some mayhem.

As was customary, there were other hired radio engineers on board, so that each could take shifts. Hiring outside engineers was common at the time. Captain Wilmott talked to the chief radio engineer on board, George White Rogers. Rogers was another engineer that had been put on notice to be fired. Though the captain didn't know that, he didn't trust Rogers, and no one on the crew seemed to like him. But the captain couldn't go around distrusting everyone, so he told Rogers to keep an eye on his assistant, Alanga. When the captain told Rogers, Rogers didn't seemed shocked; instead he told the captain that he had found two stink bomb vials in Alanga's locker, but instead of keeping them, Rogers had thrown them overboard. The story was a bit far-fetched, but the captain shrugged it off and accepted his story, now keeping his eye on Rogers as well. What no one on board knew was that Rogers had a criminal record dating back to the age of thirteen that included equipment theft and suspected arson, which was why the Ward Company was planning to terminate him.

On the cold, wet, dreary morning of September 7, the waves were beginning to pound the ship, keeping the passengers indoors. Cruise director Robert Smith decided to keep the passengers entertained with a competitive game called "Lifeboat." The premise was pretty simple. He would break the passengers into teams. Then he'd set out a signal, and the passengers would rush to their cabins, don their lifejackets, and go to their assigned lifeboats. The first team to have all their members assembled would win. The reason for this game was simple: on a previous cruise, one of the passengers had slipped on a wet floor when they were doing lifeboat drills. As a result, that passenger sued the Ward Company. To eliminate further lawsuits, Captain Wilmott suspended all lifeboat drills for passengers on the *Morro Castle*. (They were not mandatory at the time for passengers anyway, only crew members.) But Smith didn't like that "his" passengers didn't have any fire drill practice, especially because the captain had also ordered the smoke detector system turned off, stating that the smell of the salted hides cargo taken aboard from Havana would seep into the system and annoy the passengers. So Smith devised this little game as a way to circumvent the captain's suspension of drills and ensure the passengers' safety. The captain, however, learned of the game and refused permission for the passengers to play it, fearing another lawsuit. Smith had to come up with another way to entertain the guests. But he didn't have to do it for long. The waves were getting higher and rougher and more passengers were getting seasick and retiring to their cabins. Whether it was the sea or just his general overall suspicions, the captain wasn't feeling very well himself. He decided to lie down in his cabin before the captain's farewell dinner that night, where he'd have to be the ultimate host to all the passengers. This was the big party night and despite the raging seas, the passengers looked forward to it.

While the passengers were waiting for dinner, there was another man on board who was equally annoyed by the lack of safety and decided to take notes. The man, Arthur Spender, was a licensed first mate turned night watchman. He was compiling a safety report naming all of the potential disasters that could occur because of safety violations. The most important thing he noticed was that the Lyle gun, a device used in emergencies that throws a line, and is easily set off with a small explosive charge, had been removed from the bridge where it was supposed to be kept and was now for some unknown reason stored above the ceiling in the first class writing room. He found it odd, but left it there and just took notes.

The dinner began, and anticipation for the captain's arrival was high. The clock ticked on, but there was no sign of the captain. Many figured he was going to make a fashionably late entrance, as the "celebrity" of the night. But as time went by and he did not arrive, the guests became restless. Fourth Officer Howard Hanson said he remembered seeing the captain eating from a dinner tray around 8:45 in his cabin. Both Hanson and First Mate William Warms went to check on the captain. It was around 9:00 p.m. It was then they discovered why the captain was late: He was dead. They found him slumped over the bathtub with his pants around his ankles.

Just then, Chief Engineer Abbott walked in the room. He needed to tell the captain that there was a problem with one of the boilers, and that he had decided to shut it down, which would have an effect on the ship's speed. It also would affect the water pressure throughout the ship. But obviously Abbott could not deliver the message. The captain was already blue with the pallor of death.

Dr. De Witt Van Zile, one of the three ship's doctors, examined the body and determined that the captain had died of a heart attack and "nervous stomach." The other two doctors reluctantly agreed. They wanted to have an autopsy done, but seeing as they were out at sea, that wasn't possible. After some inquiry, they found out that the captain had ordered dinner to be brought to his cabin. Shortly after eating, he complained again of stomach cramps. Soon after, he died. As they dressed and moved the body, Hanson noted that the body was now turning black. He commented that that could be the result of a heart attack or food poisoning.

The death of the captain now moved Chief Officer Warms up the ladder of command. He had a thirty-five-year career at sea and had been in charge of several ships in the past, but had always been demoted for failure to follow safety regulations. The last ship he was in charge of mysteriously caught fire. Although a capable captain, he was now suddenly in charge of a ship he knew very little about in the middle of a nasty storm.

His first order was for Abbott to seal off the room. Abbott and Warms hated each other, but out of respect for the captain, Abbott listened.

It was cruise director Robert Smith's job to tell the passengers of the captain's death. They were told they were in the capable hands of Captain Warms. But were they? They were nervous, and rightfully so. A new man was at the helm, there was a dead captain on board being held in a freezer somewhere, and there was a terrible storm rocking the ship. And now each officer on the ship was in a new, unfamiliar position: If something happened, would they know what their new responsibilities would be? The passengers were now very sorry that they didn't get to play the "Lifeboat" game.

With the sullen news, many passengers retired to bed early. Others were still focused on getting as drunk as they could and partying all night long. After all, this would be the last night for some time when they could legally imbibe.

At midnight, the New Jersey shore could be seen on the port side of the ship. Soon the chief officer would be preparing to change course and get the ship into the New York Channel.

At 2:50 a.m., with the winds gusting outside at sixty miles per hour, stewards Daniel Campbell and Sydney Ryan were cleaning up some glasses from the late night partiers. They smelled smoke and thought it might be the partiers enjoying a cigarette in the passenger lounge. They went to check it out, and instead noticed smoke coming from the highly flammable first class writing room on B deck, a room filled with paper for the passengers to write messages and letters. Within minutes they found the fire in a closet in the writing room. This closet was filled with blankets that had been dry cleaned using highly flammable dry cleaning fluids. It was already engulfed in flames.

About the same time, Harold Foersch, a night watchman, reported to Captain Warms that he had seen smoke coming from a ventilator. The captain ordered Second Officer Hackney to investigate the situation quickly. Hackney soon joined the stewards.

They tried to put out the fire with an extinguisher, but it had little effect. Instead of continuing to try to put it out, Hackney ran to the phone, leaving the door to the locker closet open. He reported to the bridge what was happening and urged them to awaken the rest of the crew.

The automatic trip wires that were designed to close the doors when a certain temperature was reached had been disconnected. By the time Hackney came back, the oxygen from the open door had made the fire spread. The crew at the scene tried to control the fire, but it now had spread too far. The bridge was told the fire was out of control.

Warms had no choice but to sound the crew alarm. But the alarms had been turned off. Those crew members who were already awake now rushed to the forty-two fire hydrants on board. Not wanting to take any chances, they uncoiled the hoses and opened all the valves so they could douse the fire. But to their surprise, practically no water came out. There was no pressure in the hoses. They opened more hoses to see if those would work, but it only made the situation worse. What the untrained crew did not know was that the ship was built in such a way that only a maximum of six hoses could work at a time with full water pressure. Plus, Abbott had earlier shut off one of the boilers, further lowering the water pressure. The situation was growing worse by the minute. This time, though, no one stopped to call the bridge.

Chief Engineer Abbott was told of the situation. His job required that he don his overalls and head down to the engine room. Instead he put on his dress uniform, went to the bridge, and refused to obey more orders.

The new acting captain, Chief Officer Warms, who already had his hands full from the original captain's death and the raging seas, thought that the fire was being taken care of. The last thing he needed was people not doing their jobs.

The first rule during a fire on board a ship is to position the ship in the wind where the flames have the shortest distance to go over the side. Warms turned the *Morro Castle* into the wind, but he kept it there too long and went too fast. His plan was to go full speed ahead to get them to shore. What he didn't realize was that when he changed the direction of the boat, he also changed the direction of the fire, and the more he sped, the more the winds fed the flames. The winds spread the fire quickly through the ship decorated with highly flammable materials, the carpets and wood paneling covered heavily with veneered finish. At one point he heard a small explosion. It was the Lyle gun that had been stashed in the ceiling. The gun caused the seamen to panic, and they started throwing objects overboard in case they would need them later to float on.

The fire then spread along the wood-lined, six-inch opening between the wooden ceiling and steel bulkheads. In essence, this provided a flammable pathway that bypassed any and all fire doors, even if they had been closed. Add to this that even though the ship had fire detectors, they were only located in the ship's staterooms, crew quarters, office, cargo holds, and engine rooms. There were no detectors in the passenger areas. Had the detectors been in place, as soon as the fire started in the writing room, the crew would have been notified. Without the warning system, there was no way to let the bridge know about the fire, other than by personal messenger.

Finally word got to the bridge that the fire was out of control. A second alarm was then sounded, this time to wake the passengers. But the fire alarm produced only a "muffled, scarcely audible ring" so many did not hear it at first. At the captain's orders, crew members knocked on doors to wake passengers up. For those who did hear it, there was now utter confusion. The passengers weren't sure even where their lifeboat stations were. They were tired. Some were drunk, others hung over. The fire and smoke was choking and blinding them from making logical decisions. Those who knew that the lifeboats were in the center of the boat were blocked by the approaching flames. Most of the passengers were forced by the fire to the back, the stern of the burning ship, left helpless with no escape. Many began to pray; some started to sing.

At about 3:10 a.m. the fire burned the main electric cable, leaving the ship in total darkness and leaving Captain Warms up on the bridge with a wheelhouse and no ability to steer the ship. The boat was being tossed around like an oversized toy in the raging waves and piercing wind. Warms tried to remain calm as the heat continued to rise. He had to act. He yelled to Chief Engineer Abbott to try to get more pressure to the hoses. Abbott tried to explain to the crazed captain that it was too late, but the captain wasn't listening.

During this time, the "dangerous" radio assistant, Alanga, was on duty in the radio room two floors above the writing room. He woke up Rogers and asked if they should send out an SOS. Rogers told him to go to the bridge and get permission from Captain Warms. Alanga went up, but Captain Warms didn't know who Alanga was and ignored him. Frustrated, Alanga went back to the radio room and told Rogers that it was a madhouse up there and no one knew what they were doing. Rogers again sent Alanga up there to get permission. By now the radio room was filling with smoke and the metal floor was heating up. In order to stay near the radio, Rogers had to sit on his desk with his feet off the floor so that the soles of his shoes wouldn't melt. Over the broadcast system, Rogers could hear other ships in the area radioing the Coast Guard. The room was becoming an inferno, and sulfuric acid from the batteries that powered the transmitters had exploded and was seeping onto the floor. Finally, at 3:18, Alanga ran down with the permission from the captain to transmit the SOS. Rogers had already taken it upon himself to send out a standby call to keep the airwaves open. It was now 3:23 a.m. It had been over a half hour since the fire started, and they were just then sending out an SOS. It went out: "SOS MORRO CASTLE. A FIRE 20 MILES SOUTH OF SCOTLAND LIGHT. NEED IMMEDIATE ASSISTANCE." As he was sending out the message, the table caught fire. Rogers remained calm and kept transmitting with a steady devotion to getting his job done. This was his chance to come out a hero and secure his job.

Meanwhile, the fire had trapped some people inside their cabins. Some crew members broke windows in an attempt to help trapped passengers but, in doing so, let in the high winds from outside, which only spread the fire faster.

Captain Warms was trying everything in his power to get the ship to shore, but without a wheel to steer the ship it was very difficult. He tried to use the engines to steer, but the men down in the room said it was unbearable down there, and requested permission to leave their posts. They were just five miles off shore, near the coast of Manasquan; he knew he couldn't chance it any longer. He ordered the men to shut down the ship and drop anchor. With the shore not too far away, his hope was that people would make it to shore in the lifeboats. He left the bridge to see what was happening below. It was then he saw the pandemonium.

Most of the crew members had left their posts and were only concerned with saving themselves. Since they had participated in the fire drills, they headed toward the forecastle (toward the bow), donned life vests, jumped overboard, and left the passengers to figure it out for themselves. Other crew members ran for the lifeboats and had them lowered with only fellow crew members on board, as children and the elderly ran screaming about in panic.

One such selfish crew member was Chief Engineer Abbott. As soon as he got the chance, he put on a lifejacket, ran for a lifeboat, and ordered it lowered. There were only eight people on the boat, but there was room for sixty-three. Abbott didn't care. He was on the boat and wanted it in the water and away from the floating inferno. Captain Warms saw what was happening and ordered the lifeboat to wait for others to get on board.

Abbott refused to listen and the lifeboat was lowered in the water. As the lifeboat was lowered, Abbott ripped off the bars and gold braids from his uniform, so no one could identify him. As soon as the lifeboat hit the water, the other seven crew members on board started to row to shore. Abbott refused to help row. Instead, he watched silently as the crew rowed past floating corpses, drowning people, and people swimming for their lives using dead bodies to keep them afloat. They didn't care. Later, reflecting on what he had done, Abbott would say, "I knew I'd go to jail."

Meanwhile, as they were rowing to shore, the ship was exploding from the heat.

Windows burst and flying glass projectiles were injuring the passengers who huddled at the rear of the ship. Half the passengers didn't even have their lifejackets on, and some who did, did not know how to use them. The heat from the flames was now unbearable. The blistering deck was melting through people's shoes. They had to make a choice: jump and take their chances in the chilly, turbulent waters, or burn to death. Many chose to jump. Those who jumped and didn't have their jackets on correctly had their necks broken instantly by the force of the hard cork inside the jackets coming up on them when they hit the water. Others were sucked into the ship's propellers, as the ship had still not completely stopped.

Cruise Director Smith saw what was happening. He took control of the situation and made his way to the back of the ship to help the frightened passengers. In a calm voice, he convinced people not to jump until the propellers stopped moving. For those who didn't have lifejackets on, he helped them put them on correctly. He bandaged wounds and kept the nearby people who couldn't get to the lifeboats calm. Meanwhile, other crew members tossed floatable objects like chairs into the water so people would have things to hold onto in the storm. Some people, however, were already in the water and were knocked unconscious by objects meant to save them. When Captain Warms finally gave the official order to abandon ship, Smith did his last heroic deed. He jumped into the water with an injured woman and kept the two of them alive until help came.

The last people to abandon ship were thirteen dedicated crewmen, Captain Warms, and of all people, the two radio men, Rogers and Alanga. The two people Captain Wilmott was most suspicious of were there until the very end.

When there was no longer any hope, they leaped into the water. They were now floating waiting for rescue boats to arrive. Six lifeboats were heading toward shore. They were filled with a mere eighty-five people, most of them crew. The other six lifeboats never made it off the ship. Had everything gone smoothly, 408 people would have been in the lifeboats.

It was a while before rescue boats started to arrive. Because the SOS message got out so late, the rescuers took some time to sort through the confusion, locate the ship, and figure out what was happening.

The first on the scene was the *Andrea S. Lukenbach,* a freighter whose crew spotted the burning ship from ten miles away. She arrived at the scene at 4:00 a.m. She had only two lifeboats and was only able to rescue twenty-six people. That still left many in the water. Next was the *Monarch of Bermuda,* a British ship who was able to pluck seventy-one lucky people out of the water. The *Bermuda* was followed by the *City of Savannah,* whose crew braved the storm and was able to rescue another sixty-five who were still alive in the water. The fourth boat on the scene, the SS *President Cleveland,* made a quick circle around the burning *Castle,* saw nobody, and left the scene.

As word of the tragedy hit the media, the Coast Guard was soon joined by private pleasure boats and fishing vessels all out to help as best they could. Unfortunately, the Coast Guard ships, the *Tampa* and *Cahoone,* were too far away in the storm to see anyone in the water. It wasn't until dead bodies were reported washing up on the Jersey Shore that the Coast Guard float planes were sent in by New Jersey governor Harry Moore. Despite warnings, Moore hopped on a plane that would help nearby boats locate survivors by dropping red flag markers in the water where the bodies were.

At one point, some local radio stations started saying that everyone had already been rescued, but basing things on his experience, the skipper of the *Paramount,* a thirty-ton vessel that was on shore, decided that he should check. The *Paramount* wound up picking up sixty more survivors. The last one was a woman who had been in the water for seven hours!

Meanwhile, hundreds of good citizens flocked to the beaches to see if they could help gather victims as they floated in, those dead or alive. Those alive were sent to makeshift medical stations that were set up along the Jersey Shore from Manasquan to Sandy Hook. The dead were brought in body bags to a temporary morgue set up by the National Guard at Camp Moore.

While people were fighting for their lives, the ship itself was not ready to give up on hers either. Still anchored like a prisoner, it burned and continued to pull northward toward the Jersey Shore, dragging its anchor like a ball and chain. The Coast Guard cutter ship *Tampa* arrived. Its crew offered Captain Warms a tow for the *Morro Castle*. He agreed. The three-inch anchor had to be cut manually with a hacksaw to get it loose. It took several hours but they managed to do it. They used one of the lines hanging over the stern to help slowly tug it along toward a New York City port.

However, with the force of the hurricane-like winds and the pull of the ocean waves, the tug line snapped. The *Morro Castle* was now free to chart its own course.

The tragedy was still being reported on every radio and television station in the area. People drove to the Shore Highway, some to help, and some just to catch a glimpse of this historic event as it floated by. Then, as one radio announcer, Tom Burley of WCAP, was reporting the fate of the ship, he looked out his window from the broadcasting station in Convention Hall in Asbury Park and said, "She's here! The *Morro Castle*'s coming right towards the studio!" The blazing ship went aground mid-morning less than three hundred feet from where

Spectators look on from the shores of Asbury Park as the *Morro Castle* floats into shore unmanned on September 8, 1934.

the announcer sat. To help on land, the governor deployed an African-American unit of the state militia to patrol the beach and waters for survivors and dead bodies. Asbury Park took advantage of the opportunity to promote tourism, posting signs reading TWO MILES TO THE MORRO CASTLE WRECK and COME SEE THE MORRO CASTLE WRECK.

It was a strange mixture of emotions on the beach for the next few days. Children skipped school to see the ship. Store owners who had closed shop after Labor Day quickly reopened as they realized hordes of potential customers would be there. Amidst the tragedy, they were selling hot dogs, sodas, ice cream, and souvenirs. Bingo stands and shooting galleries were packed.

A painted banner had been put up over the convention hall, charging people 22 cents for better viewing of the burnt and twisted metal remains of the once-luxury liner. A note read that the funds would go to benefit the families of those who died. By noon, over ten thousand people had paid to get a "better view."

The ship continued to burn and smolder for seven days as the fire department desperately fought to put out the fire. Blasts from the wreck went off as they were working on it, and they feared that the flames would reach the ship's fuel tanks, which were still filled. They ordered people to stay at least three hundred feet away from the ship. The smell of dead bodies permeated the air.

It took days before any investigators or firemen could actually set foot on the heated heap.

In the end, all that was left of the once state-of-the-art, luxury cruise liner was melted solid steel plates, twisted girders, and the remaining six lifeboats that were bent as if they were tin foil. Out of the 555 souls on board (331 passengers and 224 crew), there were 137 dead, a number which included the long list of those still missing at sea. It was the largest loss of life at sea during peacetime in U.S. history.

Until March 14, 1935, when the tragic ship would be towed away and made into scrap metal, it sat there, a skeleton of what it once was. During this interim it began to take on a new life. It became a tourist attraction. Postcards and souvenirs sold well, and some visitors would even go in the water and place their hands on the ship.

Then, on September 8, 2009, seventy-five years after the *Morro Castle* tragedy, the Asbury Park Historical Society paid tribute to the first responder heroes and those who died that day. A memorial stone was placed in Asbury Park outside the convention hall at the end of Fifth Avenue across from the Paramount Theater for the entire world to see.

This tragedy will always haunt the shores of New Jersey, as will the many unanswered questions and mysteries surrounding it. The saddest thing, though, is that it all could have been avoided, even if it were arson, with some forethought, teamwork, and planning.

As Don Stine, trustee of the Asbury Park Historical Society put it, "[After] one of the most important events in American maritime history, much was changed and learned." The disaster resulted in the establishment of the Merchant Marine Academy, which would reform the requirements for licensing of the officers. Shipboard safety procedures and laws were instituted.

Several years after the disaster, a federal judge found the Ward line liable for $890,000, or $2,225 per victim. Though there were a number of theories ranging from crew incompetence to arson at the hand of Rogers, who had a string of arson cases following him, without substantive evidence the cause of the fire was never determined.

BIBLIOGRAPHY

General Sources

Martinelli, Patricia A. *True Crime: New Jersey: The State's Most Notorious Criminal Cases.* Stackpole Books, Mechanicsburg, PA, 2007.

Martinelli, Patricia A., and Charles Stansfield Jr. *Haunted New Jersey: Ghosts and Strange Phenomena of the Garden State.* Stackpole Books, Mechanicsburg, PA, 2004.

Moran, Mark, and Mark Sceurman. *Weird N.J.,* Vol. 2. Sterling Publishing Company, New York, 2006.

Sceurman, Mark, and Mark Moran. *Weird N.J.* Sterling Publishing Company, New York, 2005.

Schlosser, S. E. *Spooky New Jersey: Tales of Hauntings, Strange Happenings, and Other Local Lore.* Globe Pequot Press, Guilford, CT, 2006.

Sources by Chapter

Chapter 1—A Devil of a Son

McCloy, James F., & Ray Miller Jr. *The Jersey Devil: The 13th Child.* Middle Atlantic Press, Moorestown, NJ, 1976.

Wikipedia, Jersey Devil entry: http://en.wikipedia.org/wiki/Jersey_Devil

Chapter 2—The Friendliest Haunted Castle in New Jersey

www.artsandhealth.com/history.html

www.feldsteinfinancial.com/historypharelochcastle.html

www.southjerseyghostresearch.org/cases3/04057.html

Chapter 3—The Minister and the Choir Singer

Franklin Township Public Library Photo Archive for Hall-Mills Murders. Compiled by William B. Brahms. www.franklintwp.org/photoarchive/default .asp?SavedQuery=Hall%20and%20Mills&searchtype= boolean&sc=&RankBase=&CurrentPage=3

"James Mills, Husband of Victim in '22 Hall-Mills Slaying Dies . . ." *New York Times,* November 9, 1965, page 43.

Kunstler, William. *The Hall-Mills Murder Case: The Minister and the Choir Singer.* Rutgers University Press, New Brunswick, NJ, 1980.

"Miss Charlotte Mills, Daughter of One of the Victims in the Sensational Hall-Mills Murder Case . . ." *New York Times,* February 4, 1952, page 11.

Tomlinson, Gerald. *Fatal Tryst.* Home Run Press, Lake Hopatcong, New Jersey, 1999.

Thurber, James. "A Sort of Genius." *The Mammoth Book of Unsolved Crimes.* Carroll & Graf, New York, 1999.

Tru TV: www.trutv.com/library/crime/notorious_murders/family/mills/1.html

Wikipedia, Hall-Mills murder case entry: http://en.wikipedia.org/wiki/Hall-Mills_murder_case

"Willie Stevens, 70, of Hall-Mills Case; Eccentric Figure of Murder Trial Dies . . ." *New York Times,* December 31, 1942, page 15.

"Woman's Story Unshaken; Saw "Glistening Thing" in Broker's Hand . . ." *New York Times,* August 14, 1926, page 1.

Chapter 4—The Darker Side of Thomas Edison

About.com, Thomas Edison entry:
http://inventors.about.com/library/inventors/bledison.htm

Miskell, John N. *Executions in Auburn Prison, 1890–1916.*
Auburn, NY.

Moran, Richard. *Executioner's Current. Thomas Edison,
George Westinghouse and the Invention of the Electric Chair.*
Alfred A. Knopf, New York, 2002.

Moran, Dr. Richard. "The Strange Origins of the Electric
Chair." *Boston Globe,* August 2, 1990.

Wachhorst, Wyn. *Thomas Alva Edison. An American Myth.*
The MIT Press, Cambridge, MA, 1981.

Wikipedia, George Westinghouse entry: http://en.wikipedia
.org/wiki/George_Westinghouse

Chapter 5—The Devil's Bathtub

Beck, Henry Charlton. *More Forgotten Towns of Southern New
Jersey.* Dutton & Co. Inc, New York, 1937.

Map to Blue Hole: www.angelfire.com/nj/becjosh/bluemap.html

Video about Blue Hole: www.angelfire.com/nj/becjosh/trek.html
and www.angelfire.com/nj/becjosh/beck/beckbook.html

Walsh, Daniel. "Getting to the Bottom of the Myths of the Blue Hole in the Pine Barrens." *Courier-Post.* (New Jersey). February 7, 2003.

Chapter 6—The Insane Ghosts of Overbrook Asylum

Abandoned but Not Forgotten: www.abandonedbutnot forgotten.com/essex_county_hospital_history.htm.

"Huston's Film Set Haunted," WENN News, August 31, 2008, http://www.imdb.com/news/ni0558946.

Paranormalstories.blogspot.com: http://paranormalstories .blogspot.com/2009/04/essex-county-mental-hospital.html.

Verona-Cedar Grove Times (Newspaper). http://66.132.218.27/ NC/0/47.html.

Weird New Jersey Web site: www.weirdnj.com/index.php? option=com_content&task=view&id=230&Itemid=28.

Welcome to Nowhere: www.welcometonowhere.com/hidden/ abandoned/salvaged/further_story.html.

Chapter 7—Housewives of Essex County

Hauntings at Sanatorium Web site: www.mountainsanatorium .net/hauntings.htm.

Logbook of Patients for Sanatorium Web site: http:// mountainsanatorium.net/cgi-bin/yabb/YaBB.pl.

Mountain Sanatorium Web site: www.mountainsanatorium
.net/history.htm.

Wikipedia, Verona, New Jersey entry: http://en.wikipedia.org/
wiki/Verona,_New_Jersey.

Chapter 8—The Walking Dead of Gully Road

Hine, C.G. *Hine's Annual,* Woodside, New Jersey, 1909.

The Ghosts of Gully Road: www.njhm.com/gullyroad.htm.

NYPL Research Libraries Web site:
www.archive.org/stream/woodsidenorthend00hine/
woodsidenorthend00hine_djvu.txt.

Ranken, Edward S. *Indian Trails and City Streets.* Globe Press,
Montclair, NJ, 1927.

Chapter 9—The Boogeyman of Westfield

Benford, Thomas B., and James P. Johnson. *Righteous Carnage:
The List Murders.* iUniverse, 1991 and 2000.

Hepp, Rick. "Notorious Killer John List Dies." Newhouse
News Service, *Michigan News,* March 25, 2008.

List, John E. *Collateral Damage: The John List Story.* iUniverse,
Inc., 2006.

Ramsland, Katherine. *Straight to Hell.* TruTV.com: www.trutv
.com/library/crime/notorious_murders/family/list/1.html.

Rothman, Carly. "Body of Killer John List Remains
Unclaimed." *The Star-Ledger* (New Jersey), March 25, 2008.

Ryzuk, Mary S. *Thou Shalt Not Kill.* Warner Books, New
York, 1990.

Sharkey, Joe. *Death Sentence: The Inside Story of the John List
Murders.* Signet, New York, 1990.

Wikipedia, John List entry: http://en.wikipedia.org/wiki/
John_List.

Chapter 10—The Robin Hood of the Pine Barrens

Blackwell, Jon. *Notorious New Jersey: 100 Tales of Murders,
Mobsters and Scandals.* Rutgers University Press, New
Brunswick, NJ, 2007.

Boucher, Jack E. *Absegami Yesteryear.* Atlantic County
Historical Society, 1963.

Curtis, Eric. "Long Ago's Not Far Away." *Holiday Magazine.*
March 1946, Vol. 1, No. 1, www.biemiller.com/batsto.htm.

Joe Mulliner: www.mapsurfer.com/boxes/box35.html.

New Jersey History's Mysteries: www.njhm.com/stories.htm.

Chapter 11—The Dreaded Voyage of the *Morro Castle*

Alderson, Michael. Photos and Info on *Morro Castle*: www
.wardline.com/page/page/4878736.htm.

Burton, Hal. *The Morro Castle—Tragedy at Sea.* The Viking
Press, New York, 1973.

Gallagher, Thomas. *Fire at Sea: The Mysterious Tragedy of the*
Morro Castle. Lyons Press, Guilford, CT, 2003.

Thomas, Gordon, and Max Morgan Witts. *Shipwreck—*
The Strange Case of the Morro Castle. Dorset Press, New
York, 1972.

INDEX

Mount Pleasant Cemetery, 93, 95–96
Mullica River, 118
Mulliner, Joe, 117–27
Muybridge, Edward, 48

N
Nesco, 124–25
Nescochague Lake, 124
New Jersey Devil, 1–8, 57–64
Newark, 89–96
Newark City Home for Girls, 76
Nowenok, Chief, 9

O
Old Tuckerton, 120
Orange Mountain, 75–88
Ormsby, Bob, 64
Overbrook Asylum, 65–74

P
Payne, Phil, 39
Peterson, Fred, 52
Phareloch Castle, 9–19
Pine Barrens, 1–5, 57–64
Pine Towns, 120
Pinelands, 1–5, 57–64
Pleasant Mills, 118, 124, 127
Preith, Mrs. Edwin A., 75–88

Q
Quaker Bridge, 120, 123

R
Rastall, Catherine, 41–42
Read, Honore, 123–24
Richards, Jesse, 126
Ridley, Susan, 17, 19
Riehl, Arthur, 39
Rogers, George White, 132–33, 140–41, 144
Rowe, Mary, 92–93
Russell, Nellie, 37–38
Ryan, Sydney, 137

S
Schneider, Ray, 20–21, 32–33
Schwartz, Edward, 41
Scotts Landing, 1–4, 8
Second Mountain, 76
Sheridan, Barbara, 107
Simpson, Alexander, 39–44
Simring, Steven, 113–14
Smith, Robert, 133–34, 136, 144
Somerset County, 20
Somserset County, 22
Sopranos, The, 88
South Jersey Ghost Research Team (SJGR), 17–18
Spender, Arthur, 134
Steryker, Edward, 21
Stevens, Harry, 33
Stevens, Henry, 37, 42–43, 44, 45
Stevens, Willie, 33–45
Stine, Don, 150
Sutphen, Samuel T., 24
Sutphen, William, 39
Swan, Joseph, 48

T
Tennyson, Augusta, 28
Tesla, Nikola, 48–50, 51
Totten, George D., 22, 23
Tracy, Barnard, 112
tuberculosis, 75–88
Tumultry, Peter, 39

U
Utopia Castle, 10

V
Verona, 65

W
Walter, Richard, 111
Warms, William, 132–46
Washington, 120, 121–22
Watchung Mountain, 9
Westfield, 97
Westinghouse, George, 51, 52, 54–56

ABOUT THE AUTHOR

Fran Capo is a comedienne, spokesperson, adventurer, radio host, voice-over artist, freelance writer, and the author of thirteen additional books, including *It Happened in New Jersey* (Globe Pequot). A five-time world record holder, Fran is known as the *Guinness Book of World Records*'s fastest-talking female. She is also the co-host of the television show *Live it Up!* and a motivational speaker who lectures around the world for Fortune 500 companies, corporate promotional events, schools, and fund-raisers with her *Dare to Do It, Creativity in Marketing, Humor in Business Speaking,* and *Success Made Simple* talks and teleseminars. She has been heard on over 375 television shows and 3,500 radio shows. She also writes a weekly blog, "Adventure Mom," for Traveling Mom. Email her at FranCNY@aol.com, follow her on Twitter or Facebook, or go to her Web site, www.francapo.com, to get her monthly newsletter.